The St. Lawrence River

History, Highway and Habitat

By Janice Hamilton

Price-Patterson Ltd.

COVER PHOTO:
A farm overlooks the broad St. Lawrence River near St. Irénée
in the Charlevoix region of Quebec.

PAGE 1 PHOTO:
Tour boats are tied up in Tadoussac harbour in the late afternoon.

Library and Archives Canada Cataloguing in Publication

Hamilton, Janice
    The St. Lawrence River : history, highway and habitat / Janice Hamilton.

Includes bibliographical references and index.
ISBN 1-896881-71-8

    1. Saint Lawrence River. I. Title.

FC2756.H348 2006   971.4   C2006-901440-X

ISBN: 1-896881-71-8

Design: Studio Melrose / Ted Sancton

Printed and bound in Canada

Redlader Publishing is a division of:
Price-Patterson Ltd.
Canadian Publishers – Montreal, Canada
www.pricepatterson.com

TABLE OF CONTENTS

This cheerful field of dandelions is near Métis on the lower estuary.

DEDICATION

This book is dedicated to the memory of my father,
Jim (Dr. James D.) Hamilton,
with whom I first sailed down the St. Lawrence River
aboard the Cunard liner *Franconia* in 1963.

JANICE HAMILTON
MONTREAL, 2006

The River and Its Estuary

Stand on the Plains of Abraham in Quebec City. Just down the road are the solid grey stone walls that surrounded the old capital of New France. Beyond the city the ancient, rugged hills of the Canadian Shield fade blue into the horizon, and at your feet, a broad, straight river flows gracefully toward its destiny with the sea. This is the St. Lawrence, third largest river in North America (after the Mississippi and Mackenzie), on its way to the Atlantic Ocean from its source in the Great Lakes.

The St. Lawrence courses northeast from the heart of the continent, draining a vast basin of more than 1.3 million square kilometres (502,000 square miles), to the Gulf of St. Lawrence, where it merges with the Atlantic. Near its source it is headstrong and exuberant, pointing like an arrow towards its destination. As it reaches the end of its voyage, it matures and expands to more than 50 kilometres (30 miles) in width. No wonder the people who live

A view of the St. Lawrence River.

In Ogdensburg, New York, the U.S. Coast Guard Auxiliary Patrol prepares to make the rounds along the international border. Prescott, Ontario, is just across the river.

on the lower St. Lawrence River call it *la mer* – the sea.

It is full of mysteries and surprises. There are submerged reefs and dangerous currents, hundreds of enchanting islands and unpredictable weather. Tributaries, tides and the mixture of salt and fresh water, as well as the combination of shallow lakes, turbulent rapids and deep trenches create diverse aquatic habitats for a variety of plants and animals.

It is the cradle of Canadian history, launching spot for the exploration of North America and site of landmark battles. Today, it is a vital transportation route that provides the shortest shipping route between the industrial heartland of North America and Europe. Busy communities line its banks as it passes through Ontario and New York State, and about 60 per cent of the

people of the province of Quebec live near its shores. But people have taken the St. Lawrence for granted for centuries and allowed it to become polluted. Although clean-up efforts are beginning to pay off, many species of plants and animals that live in or near the water are still in danger of disappearing.

The St. Lawrence is a waterway of great natural beauty, and its currents and creatures, its role in history, and its impact on the economy and culture are worth a closer look.

Slicing Through the Heart of the Continent

The St. Lawrence River is the sole outlet of the Great Lakes, the largest combined body of fresh water in the world. The Great Lakes drainage basin takes in some of the most heavily populated and industrialized cities on the continent,

A clock tower marks the entrance to the Old Port of Montreal, while downtown office towers and Mount Royal rise in the background.

including Toronto, Ontario; Chicago, Illinois and Detroit, Michigan.

Measured from the western tip of Lake Superior to the Gulf of St. Lawrence, the St. Lawrence River is 3,260 kilometres (2,025 miles) long. The river proper, which begins at the outlet of Lake Ontario, is a less impressive 780 kilometres (485 miles) in length. What it lacks in length, however, is made up by volume: fed by countless streams and tributaries, the river broadens and swells until the opposite shore is no longer visible.

On the political map, the first stretch of the St. Lawrence forms the international border between the province of Ontario, Canada, and New York State, in the United States. Then the river enters the province of Quebec and remains there for the rest of its journey.

The upper St. Lawrence, from Lake Ontario to Quebec City, flows through one of the most densely populated regions of Canada. In contrast, the lower St. Lawrence – the vast tidal estuary downstream from Quebec City – is sparsely populated. Along the north shore of the lower St. Lawrence, scattered villages punctuate the wilderness, while a ribbon of farms, villages and towns extends along the south shore.

The St. Lawrence makes its way through three different geographic regions. The upper part of the river passes through the St. Lawrence Lowlands, a flat zone with rich farmland. Downstream from Quebec City, rocky headlands, peat bogs and sandy dunes along the river's north shore comprise the edge of the Canadian Shield, the highland region of Precambrian rock, formed between 4 billion and 1 billion years ago, that

The north shore of the estuary, pictured here near Port au Persil in the Charlevoix, belongs to the rugged Canadian Shield.

The gentle farmland along the south shore of the estuary is part of the Appalachian geological region.

makes up almost half of the land surface of Canada. In this region, hardy conifers are harvested for pulp and paper mills, but the soil is too thin for intensive agriculture.

The south shore of the lower St. Lawrence is part of the Appalachian Region, a belt of uplands and mountains that stretches from Newfoundland to Quebec and south through the eastern United States. Here, low terraces rise from the water's edge, and mixed forests and farmland stretch back to the hills. Deep under the riverbed, a geological fault called Logan's Line is the dividing line between the Canadian Shield and the Appalachian regions.

The river itself has four sections, each with characteristics determined by salt content and tidal activity: the fluvial section, the fluvial estuary, the upper estuary and the lower estuary. The word fluvial is defined as "referring to a river," which might seem redundant, but the upper, freshwater section of the river is very distinct from the broad salty tidal estuary.

The Fluvial Section

The fluvial section – the 240-kilometre (150-mile) stretch of water between Lake Ontario and the outlet of Lake St. Pierre – is characterized by alternating narrow, fast-flowing rapids and slow-paced, shallow lakes, including Lake St. Francis, Lake St. Louis and Lake St. Pierre.

Tibbetts Point Lighthouse at Cape Vincent, New York, signals the river's starting point. At the eastern outlet of Lake Ontario, the current picks up its pace to pass through a maze of islands, shoals and channels known as the Thousand Islands (actually, there are more than 1,700 islands and islets) that stretch from Kingston, Ontario to Brockville, Ontario and Morristown, New York. These islands – outcroppings of pink granite from a geological formation known as the Frontenac Arch, a small arm of the Canadian Shield – have been a resort area for several generations of Americans and Canadians. Summer cottages perch on many islands, but some islets are only large enough to support a few trees.

In this international section of the St. Lawrence, towns such as Alexandria Bay, Ogdensburg and the industrial city of Massena are located on the American side of the river, while Gananoque, Brockville, Prescott and Cornwall are the largest communities on the Canadian side.

Between Lake Ontario and Lake St. Pierre, the river drops 68 metres (223 feet). Several stretches of rapids once punctuated this downhill run, but most of the white water has been drained by diversions or submerged under Lake St. Lawrence, an artificial lake created in the 1950's by the construction of a massive hydroelectric power dam. The Moses-Saunders Dam near Cornwall, Ontario, and Massena, New York, jointly owned by the New York Power Authority and Ontario Power Generation, harnesses the St. Lawrence to generate about 2,000 megawatts of power for customers in Ontario and New York State.

The Ontario side of the St. Lawrence is easily explored along County Road 2, a world away from the four-lane Highway 401 with all its high-speed trucks and traffic. The old riverside road meanders past cottages, boathouses and shallow bays where water birds nest in spring. Century-old homes line the streets of quiet towns such as Iroquois and Prescott, while large commercial vessels steam up and down the nearby St. Lawrence Seaway, the system of locks and waterways that allows ships to travel between Montreal and the Great Lakes.

In the Cornwall-Massena area the Mohawk nation of Akwesasne straddles the river. This native community was here long before the

This small island near Gananoque is peaceful on an early spring morning.

Cottages and boat houses line the shore of Lake St. Francis near Cornwall, Ontario.

The Beauharnois power station generates enough electricity to power the equivalent of 310,000 homes.

A ship tied up at Montreal can be seen from the south shore of the St. Lawrence.

Europeans arrived. Today, although divided between sections in the United States and Canada, the community administers itself as a whole, and many Mohawks do not recognize the legitimacy of the international border. The ease with which people can cross the St. Lawrence in this area has encouraged some people to smuggle cigarettes and other items between the United States and Canada.

East of Cornwall the river passes through a natural lake, known as Lake St. Francis in primarily English-speaking Ontario and *Lac Saint-François* in mainly French-speaking Quebec. As the river leaves the lake, 80 per cent of the water is diverted into the 1,658-megawatt Beauharnois power generating station. The remaining water follows the river's natural course, but several stretches of rapids that once churned between Lake St. François and Lake St. Louis have virtually disappeared. Only the vestiges of locks at Coteau du Lac and the old Soulanges Canal, west of Montreal, reveal the fact that this was once a turbulent stretch of water and a busy transportation corridor.

As the St. Lawrence passes through the Montreal archipelago, its main current flows south of the island of Montreal. To the north, the Rivière des Prairies and the Rivière des Mille Îles surround the suburban city of Laval.

The Ottawa River, the St. Lawrence's first major tributary, joins the St. Lawrence at the northwest end of the Montreal archipelago. Farms and small towns line its shores, and Ottawa, Ontario (Canada's capital city) is located about 160 kilometres (100 miles) upstream. The pretty Chateauguay River is a smaller tributary that drains the southwestern corner of Quebec.

With a total population of about 3.4 million people in the Montreal region, spread through municipalities such as Westmount, Laval and south-shore Longueuil, and including 1.8 mil-

Seaway traffic passes close to the shore in Brockville, Ontario.

The St. Lawrence Seaway

The St. Lawrence Seaway, which allows ocean-going vessels to sail between Montreal and the head of the Great Lakes, includes seven locks parallel to the river between Montreal and Lake Ontario, two of them on the American side. In the Great Lakes region, the Seaway consists of the Welland Canal between Lake Ontario and Lake Erie, and locks at Sault Ste. Marie, Ontario, between Lake Huron and Lake Superior.

About 90 per cent of the cargo passing through the Seaway is bulk commodities including grain, iron ore, coal and petroleum products. The most common types of general cargo are steel and machinery.

At its peak in 1977 the Montreal-Lake Ontario section of the Seaway handled 57.7 million tons of cargo, but in the 1980's Seaway traffic began to fall off. The Seaway faces stiff competition from rail transportation, and from barge services on the Mississippi. Also, Europeans buy less North American grain than in the past. The Seaway is also at a disadvantage because it is closed in winter, and because the locks are not big enough for today's massive ocean-going ships. Its facilities require maintenance and modernization.

However, things are looking up: in 2004 the Montreal-Lake Ontario section of the Seaway handled about 30.5 million tons of cargo, a 5.5 per cent increase over the previous year, and traffic increased again in 2005.

The Thousand Islands International Bridge was first opened in 1938.

A toll bridge links Prescott, Ontario, and Ogdensburg, New York.

The old Quebec Bridge is located at a narrow stretch of the river.

The ferries that carry hundreds of cars and trucks a day across the mouth of the Saguenay River near Tadoussac (where the Saguenay meets the St. Lawrence) are an essential part of Quebec's highway system.

lion people on the island of Montreal, this is Canada's second-largest urban centre, after Toronto. A modern, multicultural city, Montreal is also the second-largest French-speaking city in the world, after Paris. One of Montreal's unique features is Mount Royal, a mound of igneous rock that forms a natural backdrop to the glass, steel and granite high-rise buildings downtown. And despite all the human activity, the Lachine Rapids remain undisturbed just a few kilometres upstream from the city's downtown core.

The Montreal waterfront is a mixture of private residences and public parks, historic sites such as the Old Port (location of the first French settlement on the island) and the working wharves of Montreal's seaport. For 24 kilometres (15 miles) from the Old Port to the east end of Montreal Island, tugs nose huge container ships alongside concrete wharves, tankers empty petroleum products by pipeline into storage tanks on shore, and other vessels sit at anchor in the river, waiting for a berth in port or clearance to enter the Seaway. This large port is an important part of Montreal's economy and it serves as the hub of an efficient transportation network, less than 36 hours by road or rail from Chicago.

Downstream from Montreal the St. Lawrence broadens into Lake St. Pierre. There it snakes through an archipelago of more than 100 low-lying islands with so many channels between them that boaters can easily become lost. On the south shore of Lake St. Pierre is the small industrial city of Sorel-Tracy, usually just known as Sorel. Nearby, several tributaries join the St. Lawrence, including the Richelieu River, which has its headwaters in Lake Champlain in northern New York State and Vermont, and the Yamaska River, which drains the adjacent farmland.

This stretch of river near Pointe du Buisson, southwest of Montreal, carries far less water than it did a century ago. Most of the river's flow was diverted into a nearby canal leading to the Beauharnois power generating station.

Bridging the St. Lawrence

The first bridge to span the St. Lawrence was the Victoria Bridge at Montreal, opened in 1860, redesigned in the 1890's, and still in use today. Nearby, the Jacques Cartier Bridge, opened in 1930, is a familiar landmark to cruise ships and other vessels as they enter the harbour. The highest point of this curved structure is 104 metres (341 feet) above the water. Other crossing points in the Montreal area include the Honoré Mercier and Champlain bridges and the 6.4-kilometre (four-mile) long Louis Hippolyte La Fontaine tunnel.

Initial efforts to cross the river at Quebec City ended in disaster. Construction of a bridge began in 1900, but the engineers made a crucial design error. Just as it was nearing completion, a span twisted and the bridge collapsed, killing

Ferries shuttle commuters between Quebec City and Lévis.

75 workers. Construction recommenced, but the centre span fell as it was being hoisted into place between the two anchoring sections, and another 13 workers died. Finally opened in 1917, the Quebec Bridge is still in use as a rail and automobile bridge. This 549-metre (1,800-foot) steel span remains the longest cantilever bridge in the world.

Next to the old bridge, a modern span suspended from a pair of sleek arches carries six lanes of traffic. When it was first opened in 1970, it was called the New Quebec Bridge, but it was renamed in honour of provincial politician Pierre Laporte, who was kidnapped and murdered in October 1970 by people who wanted Quebec to separate from the rest of Canada. The Pierre Laporte Bridge is the longest suspension bridge in Canada, with a main span of 667.5

metres (2,190 feet) and a total length of 1,041 metres (3,415 feet).

The first bridge to be constructed in the international section of the river was the Thousand Islands Bridge, opened by Canadian Prime Minister William Lyon Mackenzie King and U.S. President Franklin Delano Roosevelt in 1938, and twinned to accommodate more traffic in 1959. Actually a series of five spans that hop from island to island, this bridge has a total length of 13.6 kilometres (8.4 miles).

Another multi-span structure joins Cornwall, Ontario, Cornwall Island and Massena, New York. The South Channel Bridge, opened in 1958, soars over the Seaway shipping channel, while the North Channel Bridge was completed in 1962. Originally called the Seaway International Bridge, it was renamed the Three

The tide is coming in near St. Joseph de la Rive in the Charlevoix region.

A Tidal River

Powerful tides that rise and fall twice a day on the St. Lawrence are extremely variable, affected by the river's width, bottom slope and weather conditions. A strong wind blowing with or against the direction of the tide can affect its height, for example. The largest tides on the river occur at the eastern tip of Ile d'Orléans: as the tide rises, the water is funneled into an increasingly narrow channel, so the tide is higher here than in the wider lower estuary and gulf. The tide flows more slowly at the surface than it does just seven metres (23 feet) down, and is slowest at the river bottom, while upstream of Quebec City, the tide rises faster than it ebbs. The greatest tidal range occurs in May.

The farmers who lived along the river often used the arrival of the spring tides as a sign that it was time to plant their fields. Today tides still influence life on the river. Ferry service to islands that do not have deep harbours is scheduled around high tides, and tidal currents pose hazards to unwary boaters. Meanwhile aquatic invertebrates and plants such as rockweed, as well as wetland species, thrive in wide inter-tidal zones, providing a rich supply of food for shorebirds.

Nations Crossing in 2000 in recognition of the fact that it crosses Mohawk territory.

Between the Thousand Islands and Cornwall, a toll bridge connects Prescott, Ontario and Ogdensburg, New York. There is one bridge between Montreal and Quebec City at Trois Rivières (also known as Three Rivers). The last bridge east of Quebec City does not cross the entire river, but links Ile d'Orléans with the north shore. Further downstream, ferries carry people and vehicles across the wide estuary.

The Estuary

After it leaves Lake St. Pierre, the St. Lawrence begins to merge gradually with the sea. Its 540-kilometre (335-mile) long estuary, or tidal mouth, is so vast that geographers divide it into three sections: the fluvial estuary, the upper estuary and the lower estuary.

The fluvial estuary stretches from the eastern end of Lake St. Pierre to the eastern tip of Ile d'Orléans, downriver from Quebec City. In this section, the tide makes its influence felt, at first almost imperceptibly, then gradually increasing to an average tidal range of about four meters (13 feet) at Quebec City.

The city of Trois Rivières is located at the point where the tributary St. Maurice River forms a three-pronged delta on the north shore of the St. Lawrence. The St. Maurice River has been used to transport logs for sawmills and pulp and paper plants and to generate power for more than a century. On land, this small city is linked to the larger urban centres of Montreal and Quebec City by both the four-lane Autoroute 40 and the more scenic Route 138, once known as the *Chemin du Roi* (King's Road). Built in 1737, this was Canada's first highway.

Like the water from the Ottawa and the Richelieu rivers, water from the St. Maurice maintains its own temperature and appearance

The Montmorency River joins the St. Lawrence at the foot of the spectacular Montmorency Falls, a popular tourist attraction east of Quebec City.

A large earthquake shook the Charlevoix region in 1663, causing a huge landslide and giving the village of Les Eboulements (meaning landslides) its name. The hills around the village were formed by the impact of a giant meteorite.

An Earthquake-Prone Region

Several strong earthquakes have been recorded along the St. Lawrence over the last 350 years. Earthquakes estimated at 6 or higher on the Richter scale were recorded in 1663, 1791, 1860, 1870 and 1925 downstream from Quebec City. This seismic zone, which stretches from the Charlevoix on the north shore to Rivière du Loup on the south shore, is the most hazardous in eastern Canada. Most earthquakes in this zone seem to occur under the riverbed.

The western Quebec seismic zone, which includes the urban areas of Montreal, Ottawa and Cornwall, is also an active one that poses a threat to old buildings. A 1732 earthquake caused significant damage in Montreal and a 1944 earthquake, centred mid-way between Cornwall, Ontario, and Massena, New York, damaged chimneys and structures on both sides of the river. A third seismic zone around the lower north shore of the estuary experiences frequent small events, but no large earthquakes have been reported.

A storm gathers over the estuary.

The sun sets in late afternoon in wintertime.

for some distance before mixing with the green water of the St. Lawrence. The tide helps mix the water from these sources, as it actually reverses the flow of the St. Lawrence.

The fluvial estuary is generally about three to five kilometres (two to three miles) wide, but it squeezes down to its narrowest point – 870 metres (0.5 mile) – just before it reaches Quebec City, the provincial capital. After the St. Lawrence passes the heights of the city, it suddenly widens, reaching 15 kilometres (9.3 miles) across at the eastern tip of Ile d'Orléans. Here the main flow of the river and the shipping channel pass south of the island, while pleasure boats use the shallower north channel with its view of Montmorency Falls, at 84 metres (275 feet), the highest waterfall in Quebec.

The upper estuary is the transition zone between fresh and salt water. The main characteristic of this section, which stretches from Ile d'Orléans to the mouth of the Saguenay River, is brackish water, since the rising tide brings salt water upstream, mixing it with fresh. Between Ile d'Orléans and Ile aux Coudres the water is also particularly turbid because strong currents keep a lot of sedimentary material suspended. Throughout the upper estuary, the shipping channel remains close to the north shore.

The contrast between the north and south shores in this region is startling. The south shore features pebbled beaches and shallow bays, and the shoreline Highway 132 links picturesque towns such as Montmagny, Kamouraska and Métis. Dikes protect the area's fertile, sandy farmland from flooding, and broad salt marshes are home to a variety of wildlife. The two largest cities, Rivière du Loup, an educational, administrative and commercial hub, and Rimouski, a regional government and service centre, sit astride gentle terraces beside the shore.

There is a deep channel between Ile aux Coudres and the river's north shore.

Fog shrouds a rocky beach in Bic provincial park, near Rimouski.

The landscape of the river's north shore, pictured here at Les Bergeronnes, near Tadoussac, features granite typical of the Canadian Shield.

The warm March sun begins to melt the ice along the shores of Lake St. Louis.

Ice fog rises off the river on a very cold January day.

On the north shore – a region known as the Charlevoix – the land rises dramatically from the water. Route 362 twists up and down steep hillsides to villages such as St. Joseph de la Rive and St. Irénée, tucked into tiny footholds at the water's edge, while the main Highway 138 follows the height of land. The region's two largest towns, Baie St. Paul and La Malbaie (also known as Murray Bay), are located at the mouths of short tributaries, and vast expanses of mud and rock are exposed at low tide in the adjacent bays. In fact, the name La Malbaie, which means the bad bay, is attributed to explorer Samuel de Champlain. He anchored there one evening at high tide and discovered the next morning that his ship was high and dry.

These two towns and the rivers that wind through them are located on the outer edges of a vast crater, 54 kilometres (33.5 miles) in diameter. It was formed some 350 million years ago when a 15-billion ton meteorite, two kilometres (1.25 miles) across, slammed into Earth. Part of the crater is hidden under the river, but although the semicircular form of the Charlevoix meteorite crater is visible from the air, scientists did not recognize it until 1965 when shatter cones – rocks that are associated with meteorites – were discovered in the area. A group of steep hills that reach 780 metres (2,560 feet) above sea level is at the centre of the crater.

The mouth of the Saguenay River and the adjacent village of Tadoussac mark the beginning of the lower estuary. The Saguenay flows southeast from the 104,000-square kilometre (40,000-square mile) Lac St. Jean, an industrial area where hydroelectricity powers aluminum plants and pulp and paper operations. The Saguenay River is 275 metres (900 feet) deep in places and forms a spectacular 100-kilometre long (60-mile) fjord surrounded by high cliffs.

The lower estuary of the St. Lawrence widens from 24 kilometres (15 miles) at the mouth of the Saguenay to 50 kilometres (30 miles) across at Pointe des Monts. Underwater lies the Laurentian Channel, a 300-metre (980-foot) deep valley that stretches from the mouth of the Saguenay to the continental shelf. This channel is characterized by several distinct layers of water. In summer a layer of relatively warm water lies at the surface, with an ice-cold layer in the middle and a very salty layer at the bottom. This channel draws large amounts of cold seawater into the estuary, and the tides, winds and the shape of the bottom (there is a shallow sill at the mouth of the Saguenay) cause the cold water to rise toward the surface, bringing with it nutrients and frequent fog patches.

Two large north shore tributaries, the Manicouagan and Rivière aux Outardes, flow into the lower estuary near the town of Baie Comeau, draining a vast wilderness area. Several huge hydroelectric projects, including the Daniel Johnson Dam, the largest multiple-arch-and-buttress dam in the world, harness the rivers' power, together generating about 6,800 megawatts of electricity. The Manicouagan Reservoir is unique in that it was formed by a meteorite that hit Earth more than 200 million years ago. What remains is a circular lake 70 kilometres (43 miles) across that rings a large island.

Islands of the St. Lawrence

The numerous islands that dot the St. Lawrence contribute to the river's natural beauty and cultural diversity. The river's largest island, Montreal, is in the fluvial section, as are the Thousand Islands. These include Wolfe Island, the largest of the Thousand Islands and accessible by ferry from both the Canadian and American mainland; Wellesley Island, on the American side of the river and known for its

Sunbathers seek the cool water of the Lachine Rapids to escape the heat of summer.

It is possible to spend a quiet afternoon fishing on the shore of the St. Lawrence in the borough of LaSalle, only 15 minutes from downtown Montreal.

Ile d'Orléans is known for its fertile farmland.

Ile aux Coudres was once an important shipbuilding centre, but most of the *goélettes*, or schooners, that were built here have fallen into disuse and decay.

Les Iles du Pot à l'Eau de Vie (the Brandy Pot Islands) are located near Rivière du Loup. This former lighthouse now serves as a small inn in the summer.

Victorian-style architecture; Grenadier Island, once farmed by Loyalist settlers; Mermaid Island, a favorite sunny spot for northern water snakes; and Bostwick Island, site of Half Moon Bay, where generations of families have come by skiff, small boat or dingy to attend summer church services.

Many of the river's most charming islands are in the estuary. The 190-square kilometre (73-square mile) Ile d'Orléans, the river's second largest island, is famous for its stone parish churches and farmhouses with curved roofs, typical of early French Canadian architecture. Farmers on its high, fertile plateau grow potatoes and fruit, while rocks and reefs dominate the shoreline. Geologically, Ile d'Orléans belongs to the Appalachian region, but it is connected via a suspension bridge to the nearby north shore.

Ile aux Coudres, named for the hazel trees (*coudriers*) that once grew on its plateau, is a tranquil place. A ferry to and from St. Joseph de la Rive transports residents and tourists attracted by the island's historic charm.

Scattered like links in a broken chain, several archipelagoes and islands, including Ile aux Grues, Ile aux Oies and Grosse Ile, lie close to the south shore. Further downstream are the uninhabited Iles du Pot à L'eau de Vie (the Brandy Pot Island archipelago) and nearby Ile au Lièvres, named by Champlain for its large population of snowshoe hares. Numerous shipwrecks lie in the waters around them.

Ile Verte, with a year-round human population of only 40, is a haven for seabirds. Further down the estuary is Ile aux Basques, where archaeologists have found evidence of occupation by native peoples about 1,300 years ago, and by Basque fishermen and whalers from the year 1580.

The Gulf of St. Lawrence

The Gulf of St. Lawrence is a 195,000-square kilometre (75,300-square mile) inland sea, enclosed by the lower north shore region of Quebec, the Gaspé Peninsula, Newfoundland and Labrador, and Cape Breton Island, Nova Scotia. The province of Prince Edward Island and Anticosti Island, which belongs to Quebec, are located within the gulf.

There is no obvious place where the estuary ends and the gulf begins, and different criteria can be used to define the boundary between these bodies of water. Basing the distinction on types of marine organisms puts the boundary at Pointe des Monts, so the lighthouse on that point of land 240 kilometres (150 miles) downstream from the Saguenay marks the end of the estuary and the beginning of the gulf.

Ships enter the gulf from the Atlantic Ocean through the Cabot Strait, between southwestern Newfoundland and Cape Breton Island, or through the Strait of Belle Isle, the body of water that separates the island of Newfoundland from the mainland Labrador coast. The northern route through the Strait of Belle Isle is not usually used in winter.

The Gaspé Peninsula begins on the south shore of the lower estuary and extends into the gulf. Many residents of the Gaspé live close to the coast. For centuries their livelihoods depended on the vast quantities of codfish that thrived in gulf waters, but these fish stocks have become seriously depleted, and the cod fishery was closed in 1993.

In the north shore's largest communities, Port Cartier and Sept Iles (also known as Seven Islands), many people are employed by industries based on the rich natural resources and hydroelectric power available in the area. Farther east, the lower north shore of the Gulf of St. Lawrence is, quite literally, the end of the road –

Port of Montreal personnel monitor activities from the port's main control room.

The Racine container terminal in Montreal is in operation night and day.

A laker glides through the Seaway locks at Iroquois, Ontario.

A ship makes its way along the estuary on a windless August afternoon.

on land, anyway. The highway ends at Natashquan, and residents of the isolated fishing villages in the rocky wilderness beyond have to travel by boat or plane.

The waters of the lower estuary and the gulf are a maze of complex current patterns and whirlpools, influenced by large masses of warm and cold water, dominant winds from the west, tides, the slope of the bottom and the flow of fresh water. Water descending the river toward the sea generally flows along the south shore where it mixes with icy water from the Laurentian Channel and forms a strong eastward current called the Gaspé Current. On the north shore, the Labrador Current sweeps westward along the coastline, introducing cold water from the north Atlantic. In the gulf, the volume of ocean water is twelve times greater than that of fresh water from the St. Lawrence.

Variable Weather

In general, the climate of this vast region is warm and humid in summer and cold and snowy in winter, but the St. Lawrence flows north as well as east, so climatic conditions differ considerably between its source and its mouth. Near the river's source, Lake Ontario moderates temperatures and increases wind and precipitation, especially in winter. In the Montreal region, summers are generally hot and humid, while winters tend to be cold and snowy. Winters are considerably longer and colder on the north shore east of Quebec City, and summers are also cool. On the south shore of the estuary, summers are warm and wet, while winters are often snowy.

Mariners have learned to expect the unexpected on the St. Lawrence, especially in the estuary, where squalls often develop. These sudden, violent windstorms can be accompanied by heavy rain and dense fog.

In winter, ice forms and breaks up at different times along the river. It usually begins to form during the first two weeks of December upstream of the Saguenay, and by the end of the month, much of the river is ice-covered. Along the shoreline, the ice usually stays in place, but winds and currents can keep ice drifting in the deep shipping channel all winter. The Canadian Coast Guard installs log-shaped steel ice booms in late autumn at strategic spots in Lake St. Pierre to anchor the ice in place along the shore and to help the current in the open channel maintain its swift pace. The river is usually ice-free by the beginning of April, although ice floes often remain in the Gulf of St. Lawrence until May.

Transportation Gateway

Location is the key to the river's significance for shipping. The St. Lawrence provides the shortest route between central North America and northern Europe and the Mediterranean. The river is blessed with a deep natural shipping channel as far inland as Ile d'Orléans, and the channel has been dredged between Quebec City and Montreal to accommodate large ocean-going vessels. The St. Lawrence Seaway completes the shipping route to the Great Lakes.

Container ships, packed with imports varying from furniture to fruit, sail upriver to Montreal, the largest container port in Canada. The containers are then placed on trains or trucks for transport to destinations and customers across Canada and the United States, while exports make the same journey in reverse. In 2004 the port handled more than 1.2 million such containers. Other vessels that ply the St. Lawrence include bulk carriers carrying loose products such as wine, oil, scrap metal and grain, and ships carrying general cargo that is not packed in containers.

This boat carries trained river pilots back and forth between the ships that they guide and their base at Les Escoumins, near Tadoussac.

A Canadian Coast Guard icebreaker helps to keep the river open during winter.

This Canadian Coast Guard hovercraft is breaking up ice on Lake St. Louis.

Trees in the Old Port of Montreal glow in the October sunshine. Within a week, all their leaves will have fallen off.

Long, flat lake carriers, or lakers, designed to carry bulk cargoes on the Great Lakes, the Seaway and the St. Lawrence River, are another common sight. Lakers transport iron ore from mines in northeastern Quebec and Labrador to manufacturing centres around the Great Lakes, and wheat, corn, oats, flaxseed and other agricultural products from western Canada and the United States bound for markets overseas. Many lakers are self-unloaders, with equipment in their holds that automatically raises cargo to deck level so it can be put on a conveyer belt. This is especially efficient for bulk cargoes such as salt, coal, sand, iron ore and grain, since a laker can anchor next to a giant ocean bulk carrier and rapidly unload its cargo directly into the other ship's hold.

These days cargo traffic on the St. Lawrence River, the Seaway and the Great Lakes is on the increase, due in part to a marketing campaign that promotes "Hwy H$_2$O." In the summer of 2005, tugs hauling barges loaded with wood chips and aluminum ingots appeared on the estuary for the first time since the 1970's. With skyrocketing fuel prices and truck traffic clogging highways, shipping via the marine highway is becoming more attractive. Water is the cheapest way to transport bulk goods: one ship can carry the equivalent of 250 rail cars or 600 trucks, and ships use 10 to 20 per cent of the energy required by trucks. Furthermore, proponents of marine transportation argue that it is relatively safe. The last time a serious accident occurred on the St. Lawrence was 1988, when about 500 tons of crude oil spilled into the river near Quebec City.

Ferries are a part of life on the lower St. Lawrence. Small ferries with open decks carry passengers and vehicles between the mainland and some islands, and in the broad estuary, where there are no bridges, ferries carry hundreds of cars and transport trucks across the river daily. Coastal vessels that bring supplies to isolated communities along the lower north shore also carry passengers.

In summer and autumn, cruise ships bring tourists up the scenic St. Lawrence and Saguenay. Tour boats take visitors through the Thousand Islands, where there is a fresh view around every point of land, or out into the waters of the estuary to watch for whales. Sailboats and power-driven pleasure boats appear in the summer, especially on the lakes of the fluvial section.

During the winter, ice once posed an insurmountable obstacle to shipping. Today, despite long hours of darkness, a weak winter sun and nights that can dip to minus 30° Celsius (minus 22° Fahrenheit), Canadian Coast Guard icebreakers with powerful engines and reinforced steel hulls that can withstand great pressure keep the channel open for commercial shipping.

Three mid-size icebreakers are responsible for icebreaking on the north shore of the gulf and the river as far inland as Quebec City. Sometimes during stretches of particularly cold temperatures and thick ice, or when commercial ships don't have enough horsepower to make their own way through the ice, Canadian Coast Guard icebreakers come to their assistance. Two smaller ships that can be used as either buoy tenders or as icebreakers maintain the channel between Quebec City and Montreal. Hovercraft also play a role in keeping small channels flowing and in breaking up ice jams that can cause flooding. Hovercraft are not only useful in very shallow areas, they can go on top of the ice so

A small, seasonal ferry operates on the Ottawa River, a St. Lawrence tributary, between the towns of Hudson and Oka, Quebec.

The Chaudière River Falls are located on the south shore of the St. Lawrence, near Quebec City.

The tranquil Rivière du Sud Ouest meanders through Bic provincial park on the south shore of the St. Lawrence.

A rainstorm moves across the Saguenay River near Tadoussac.

that the huge fans located underneath these vessels can create waves that break it up.

The river's busiest ports all handle international cargo. More than 22 million tons of cargo, including containerized goods, petroleum products and miscellaneous cargo, pass through the port of Montreal every year. Quebec City handles dry and liquid bulk goods, including chemical and petroleum products, and there are two passenger terminals for cruise vessels. Davie Industries, founded in 1825, has shipbuilding facilities across the river in Lévis. The Sept Iles Port Authority administers a natural, ice-free deep-water harbour. Through its facilities, iron ore from mines in northern Quebec is shipped around the world, while raw materials are imported to supply the largest aluminum smelter in North America. Port Cartier handles large vol-

umes of bulk products, such as grain and iron ore.

Submerged reefs, whirlpools, strong tidal currents and unpredictable weather present difficulties to navigators, so commercial ships are required to use professional river pilots. These pilots – often individuals who grew up in communities along the river, and whose relatives and ancestors were also mariners – have extensive knowledge of the St. Lawrence.

Shippers also rely on numerous navigational aids to assist them. The Canadian Coast Guard maintains automatically operated lighthouses, while hundreds of buoys and lighted markers indicate shipping channels. Pilots also depend on an electronic navigation system that feeds information about a vessel's location from a satellite into the ship's onboard computer.

Christian Pelletier sells fish and seafood by the roadside in Rivière du Loup during the spring and summer months.

Commercial Fishing

Fishing is not a major industry on the St. Lawrence. The Thousand Islands and Lake St. Francis are popular with sports fishermen, and there is a small commercial fresh-water fishery, mainly in Lake St. Pierre, but the commercial freshwater catch has declined due to contamination of some species, increasing scarcity of other species and changes in fish habitats.

In the lower estuary and gulf, commercial fishing provides some jobs, especially on the lower north shore and on the Gaspé coast. The catch includes snow crab, shrimp, lobster, soft-shell clams and whelk. Herring, mackerel, capelin, turbot (also known as Greenland halibut) and eel are also fished commercially. The fishing season is generally limited to the warm months between May and September.

Most villages in the Gaspé, such as Grande Vallée, are close to the Gulf of St. Lawrence.

CHAPTER TWO

Five Hundred Years and More

At first it was the river of the Iroquois. Then it became the river of fur traders, missionaries and explorers, a river of military significance, a graveyard for ships, a highway for floating timber and a gateway for immigration. More recently it has been a source of electric power, a sewer for waste and an important commercial shipping route. It has shaped the course of Canadian history, while humans changed its course when they tamed its rapids. The St. Lawrence River has been many things to many people, and it has many tales to tell.

The Great Lakes and the St. Lawrence are young bodies of water, created when the continental ice sheet that covered North America as far south as the central United States retreated

"Shooting the Rapids", painted in 1879 by Frances Anne Hopkins, evokes the spirit of the fur traders who were such a familiar sight on the St. Lawrence. Hopkins, who was married to a Hudson's Bay Company official, accompanied her husband on several canoe trips. The artist put herself and her husband into the painting as passengers seated in the middle of the canoe.

This drawing of an Iroquois man and woman is dated 1801.

the southern edge of the hard Canadian Shield, by scouring out depressions that filled with water and by damming up outlets with deposits of sand and gravel.

Around 14,000 years ago, glaciers still extended south of the modern Great Lakes region, and the runoff drained to the south. Two thousand years later, several large water bodies that were precursors to the Great Lakes had appeared, but they also drained to the south. After another 2,200 years, the ice had retreated north of the St. Lawrence valley, a valley that had been created by ancient geological fractures and faults, including Logan's Line, along the junction of the Canadian Shield and the Appalachian region. Water from Lake Ontario began to flow through this natural outlet. Meanwhile more water poured from another outlet in the upper Great Lakes into the Ottawa valley and from there into the St. Lawrence.

As water that had been locked in the ice was freed, sea levels rose and the land slowly began to spring up as the weight that had depressed it lightened. Because the land rose relatively slowly, a new feature appeared about 12,000 years ago: a vast inlet of salt water called the Champlain Sea inundated the St. Lawrence valley between Quebec City and Brockville, as well as the Ottawa valley, for a period of about 2,000 years. As the land sprang up higher, most of this water drained away into the Atlantic Ocean. Evidence of the Champlain Sea can be seen today in the fossils of marine animals that turn up on dry land and in the fertile clay soil it left behind. Deposits left by the retreating glaciers and this inland sea gently reshaped St. Lawrence valley.

Vast quantities of water continued to flow through the Ottawa valley from Lakes Superior, Michigan and Huron until about 4,700 years ago when the rising land closed off that outlet.

at the end of the last ice age. That period, known as the Wisconsin Ice Age, began about 75,000 years ago. At its peak, about 18,000 years ago, the ice was approximately three kilometres (1.9 miles) thick over the current site of Quebec City and two kilometres (1.25 miles) thick in eastern Ontario.

During the Wisconsin Ice Age, the ice sheet advanced and retreated several times, beginning its final retreat about 12,000 years ago. As the ice came and went, it redesigned the landscape, excavating valleys here, creating dams there, and depositing sand, gravel, rock and debris everywhere. This process eventually created the Great Lakes in an area of soft rock at

Gravel deposits had by then blocked access to southern rivers. Since then, water has flowed from the upper Great Lakes into Lake Huron, Lake Erie and Lake Ontario, and from there into the St. Lawrence, making the St. Lawrence River the sole outlet of all the lakes.

Aboriginal Inhabitants

Aboriginal people have inhabited the St. Lawrence River valley for thousands of years, and archaeologists have found evidence of human occupation at a number of sites. For example, stone hunting tools, discovered at the remains of a campsite on Gordon Island in the Thousand Islands, probably belonged to nomadic hunters who visited the area around 7000 B.C. There is other evidence that people fished and hunted waterfowl there around 4000 B.C. Around 1500 B.C. aboriginal nomads brought clay pots to the site, and 600 years later they had learned how to grow corn as well as fish, hunt and collect berries and nuts.

At Pointe du Buisson, west of Montreal, 3,000-year-old pottery shards, as well as arrow heads, beads and pipes are among the two million artifacts discovered so far. Nomadic people who camped here seasonally to fish for sturgeon, walleye and catfish left behind bear, deer and beaver bones. Near the mouth of the St. Pierre River, a small tributary that once flowed through downtown Montreal, archaeologists have found bits of pottery and evidence of a prehistoric hearth dating from about A.D. 570 to 1500.

There is evidence of aboriginal occupation of numerous sites along the north shore of the estuary, during both the period 8,000 to 3,000 years ago, before the introduction of pottery, and during the period 3,000 to 400 years ago when people made and used ceramic pots for cooking. These hunters came to the banks of the St.

This sketch of Micmac wigwams opposite Quebec was done by Millicent Mary Chaplin. She came to Canada with her husband, a British army captain, between 1838 and 1842.

This watercolour of natives poling up the rapids was done by Philip John Bainbrigge, a military artist posted to Canada between 1836 and 1842.

This watercolour of the Plains of Abraham and Cape Diamond at Quebec City was painted around 1793 by George Heriot.

Lawrence around Tadoussac looking for seals, and they left behind stone and bone tools, including semi-circular knives for cutting seal fat, and Iroquoian-style pottery. They also made ochre rock paintings at a site near Les Escoumins some 2,000 years ago.

When the Europeans began to explore North America in the 16th century, most of the native people they encountered along the shores of the St. Lawrence belonged to two main language groups: those who spoke dialects of Algonquian languages and those who spoke Iroquoian languages.

The aboriginal inhabitants of the lower Great Lakes, present-day New York State and the St. Lawrence Lowlands were Iroquoian-speaking. These were sedentary, agricultural people. The families of several related women lived in parti-tioned compartments of 30-metre (98-foot) long bark-covered buildings called longhouses. The longhouses were clustered in villages surrounded by wooden palisades. The women, aided by the children, gathered berries, made clothing out of animal hides, and grew corn, beans and squash. The men were warriors and were responsible for hunting and fishing. Travelling by canoes built from the bark of elm trees, the Iroquois traded and had political alliances with other aboriginal groups over a wide area of eastern North America.

The Algonquian-speaking peoples included the Algonquins, whose territory was in the vicinity of the Ottawa valley, and the Micmac who inhabited the Gaspé Peninsula. Living in small bands in winter, they followed deer and other game into the interior. In summer they gathered in larger groups along riverbanks and the seashore where fish, shellfish, birds and fruit were plentiful. They lived in conical lodges covered with bark in summer and animal hides in winter, and travelled easily by snowshoe and toboggan in winter, and by light-weight birch-bark canoe in summer.

The Innu, or Montagnais, who inhabited the north shore of the St. Lawrence northeast of Tadoussac, were part of another language group: they spoke a dialect of Cree. They survived by hunting, fishing and berry-picking, but the French knew them as successful traders.

All of these people depended on rivers and lakes, not only because it was faster and easier to travel by water than on foot trails through the thick forests, but because fish and shellfish were so essential to their diets, and they used a variety of implements for fishing, including bone fish hooks, nets, harpoons, spears and weirs.

Early Exploration

In 1497 explorer John Cabot claimed Newfoundland for King Henry VII of England and brought home stories of incredible quantities of cod in the sea. He noticed the Gulf of St. Lawrence and hoped it would be a passage to China and India.

Jacques Cartier arrived next, sent by King Francis I of France in 1534 to look for gold and other treasures, and to find a route to the spices and silks of Asia. The first European to explore the St. Lawrence River itself, he made three trips. On his first voyage, Cartier made his way through the Strait of Belle Isle, where he was disappointed to see such bleak, rocky terrain. He also sailed along the Gaspé coast where he and his men gave knives and trinkets to some Micmac they encountered. Then, faced with strong headwinds and currents near Anticosti Island, he decided to go home.

The native people taught Cartier how to cure scurvy with vitamin C-rich cedar tea.

The native people brought their year's catch to the fur trade fair in Montreal every year.

Jacques Cartier remarked on the spectacular view from the top of Mount Royal.

Returning in 1535, Cartier sailed into a bay in the estuary on August 10, the feast day of Saint Lawrence, a Christian martyr who was put to death by the third-century Roman emperor Valerian. Cartier named the bay after Saint Lawrence, but eventually the name stuck to the whole river.

Cartier has also been credited with giving both Quebec and Canada their names: Quebec comes from the Algonquian word for "the place where the river narrows" at Quebec City. The name Canada derives from a misunderstanding: when Cartier heard an Iroquois chief refer to his village as "kanata," Cartier thought the name referred to the whole region.

During that second trip, Cartier reached the Iroquois village of Stadacona, near present-day Quebec City. He also travelled as far inland as Hochelaga, an Iroquois village on the island of Montreal, and climbed the nearby mountain that he named Mount Royal, a name that the mountain bears to this day. Cartier and his men spent a harsh winter near Stadacona, and two dozen of them died of cold and disease. More would have perished from scurvy, but the Iroquois showed them how to drink tea made from the vitamin C-rich leaves and bark of the white cedar tree. When he left for France in 1536, Cartier took along several captured Iroquois.

On his third trip, in 1541-42, Cartier tried, but failed, to establish a colony. When he returned to France with a cargo of what he thought was gold and diamonds, he became a laughingstock: the minerals turned out to be worthless iron pyrite and quartz.

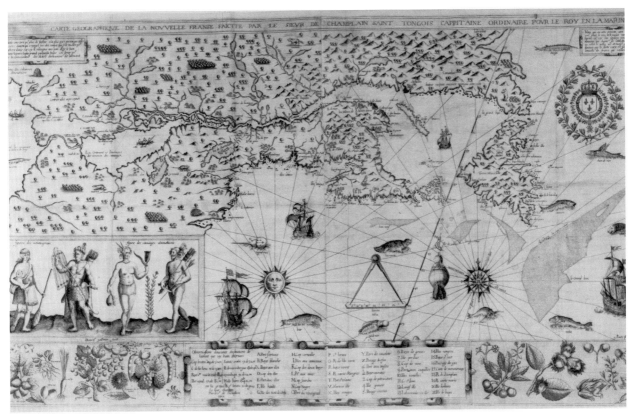

This is Samuel de Champlain's map of the St. Lawrence.

Interest in further exploration died after that fiasco, but the St. Lawrence continued to receive many European visitors: fishermen who caught the plentiful cod in the gulf, and whalers. Whales were hunted for their oil, which was used for lighting and as an ingredient in soap and other products. Each summer the whalers set up camp on the shores of Labrador and Ile aux Basques in the lower estuary and built stone ovens to boil the blubber and extract the oil. Most of the whalers were Basques, from the border area of France and Spain. The Basques became regular visitors to the gulf and estuary from about 1540 to the end of the 16th century.

Many fishermen brought European goods such as kettles, knives and blankets to trade with the aboriginal people for furs, especially beaver pelts. By 1600 Tadoussac was a busy trading centre, with up to 20 vessels anchored there each summer. The Montagnais dominated the fur trade with the French there, and the aboriginal traders travelled north to Hudson Bay and south to New England to collect the valuable skins.

In 1603 interest in the fur trade drew French explorer Samuel de Champlain to probe the river as far as the island of Montreal, where he discovered that the village of Hochelaga had disappeared. To this day no one knows what happened to it. Some historians think the inhabitants, known as the St. Lawrence Iroquois, were wiped out by European diseases, others suggest enemies drove them away.

In 1608 Champlain established the first permanent French colony in North America, a trading fort at the future site of Quebec City. He and

This drawing portrays Samuel de Champlain at the window of his *habitation* in Quebec.

A crack in the ice posed a terrifying threat to anyone trying to cross the frozen river.

his men built a *habitation* – a group of wooden buildings surrounded by walls and a moat – near the riverbank. Again the winter was hard, and the native people had to show the newcomers how to prevent scurvy. Over the next decades, Champlain continued to explore the region. He died at Quebec in 1635, but where his body was buried remains a mystery.

Champlain became known as the father of New France because of his role in establishing the French colony there. At first Quebec was merely a trading post, but gradually more settlers arrived, including missionaries and tradespeople. The newcomers founded the fur trading post they called Trois Rivières in 1634, and Ville Marie (later known as Montreal) was established in 1642 as a mission to convert the natives to Christianity.

New France and the Fur Trade

There were as yet no roads, so the St. Lawrence River became Main Street, New France. To protect the ships that carried supplies, soldiers and settlers between France and Quebec, the French were training river pilots by 1635. These men became experts who knew where every submerged rock and shifting sandbar was located.

Settlement progressed quickly, especially after King Louis XIV arranged for 800 young women to be sent to New France between 1663 and 1673. Known as *les filles du roi* (the king's daughters), they chose their own husbands from among the men of the colony and started raising the first of many generations of large families.

Members of the nobility, administrators and military officers held large properties called *seigneuries*, which they subdivided into long strips, each with a narrow stretch of riverfront. Tenants called *habitants* cleared the land. By the 1760's the shores of the St. Lawrence and

This Bainbrigge watercolour shows *habitants* fishing for shad in the St. Lawrence in May, 1840.

Fishing Methods

The *habitants* who lived along the St. Lawrence and its tributaries loved to eat fish and employed a variety of fishing methods, many of which they learned from the native people. For example, they made snares from sticks with leather or wire loops. They held the snare under the water, passed the noose over a fish and quickly jerked it out of the water. This method was used to snare salmon and for fishing through holes in the ice.

Along Lake St. Pierre, people used gill nets to catch pike and carp under the ice. They made holes in the ice about four metres (13 feet) apart and passed a net between the holes. The net was held down with rocks, and the current carried the fish into it.

Spear fishing at night was also popular. Bright torches were stuck in iron baskets at the front of the canoes, and people speared the fish that were attracted to the light. Occasionally they even caught large sturgeon in this manner. Eels were another favorite quarry; people trapped them in summer or speared them in winter when they congregated in large groups in the mud banks.

The title of this drawing by artist William Raphael was "Halfbreed Fisherman."

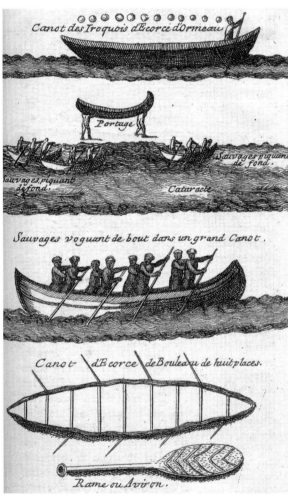

These sketches show the construction and use of the Iroquois canoe.

several of its tributaries had been settled from Ile d'Orléans to Montreal, and New France had acquired an agricultural character.

Nevertheless, fur dominated trade between Europe and North America. For more than a century, the native people brought canoes laden with fur pelts to the annual fur-trading fair on the Montreal waterfront. But many of them died of European diseases such as smallpox, to which they had no immunity, while others died in warfare. Some of the aboriginal groups had been rivals for a long time, and their differences widened with the arrival of the Europeans. The Iroquois quickly became enemies of the French and eventually allied themselves with the English to the south, while the majority of Algonquian peoples became allied with the French.

With the aboriginal population in decline, French adventurers and Canadian-born traders of European descent began to travel to the wilderness to collect furs from the native trappers. These hardy individuals were known as the *coureurs de bois* and *voyageurs*. During the mid and late 1600's, the desire to expand and control the fur trade encouraged the French to push into the interior from their base on the St. Lawrence River. Travelling by canoe, men such as René-Robert Cavelier, Sieur de La Salle and Pierre Gaultier de La Vérendrye set out from Montreal to explore vast regions of North America, from the mouth of the Mississippi to the Rocky Mountains.

In 1673 the French built a fort at the eastern end of Lake Ontario: Fort Frontenac became an outpost against the hostile English and their Iroquois allies, a mission and trading post, and future site of Kingston, Ontario.

During the fur-trade era Quebec was the most important port on the river. Large sailing vessels had difficulty reaching Montreal, not only because Lake St. Pierre was so shallow, but also because a strong current just below the Montreal waterfront sometimes forced ships to wait for days until the wind was strong enough to push them into port. Montreal, meanwhile, was the capital of the fur trade and the launching point for travellers headed into the interior.

To reach the interior, the French fur traders, missionaries and explorers favoured a route that followed the Ottawa River, rather than the St. Lawrence, partly because the hostile Iroquois controlled the latter. Also, travellers had to portage around the rapids on the upper St. Lawrence, carrying all their baggage and canoes along the shoreline for several kilometres at a stretch. Maps made as late as the mid-1700's indicate the colonists knew few details about the St. Lawrence River above Montreal.

A 1757 report on navigation in Canada indicated that travel through the gulf and estuary was still very dangerous. One reason the French did not publish good charts was because they regarded these natural hazards as a defence against would-be attackers. New France was a huge territory, and the French and British struggled for control of this highly desirable prize. Fighting broke out in 1754 in what became known in America as the French and Indian War. The broader, European phase of this conflict was called The Seven Years' War (1756-1763). The Battle of the Plains of Abraham, fought on a farmer's field beside the colonial capital of Quebec on September 13, 1759, was the decisive battle as far as the future of New France was concerned. Many Quebecers remember these events as *la guerre de la conquête* – the war of the conquest.

Before the battle, the French and their military leader, General Louis-Joseph Montcalm, felt secure. The town was built in an easily defended location on a promontory overlooking the river.

Built in 1747, the Little Chapel of Tadoussac, also known as the Indian Chapel, is the oldest wooden church in Canada.

This old house on Ile d'Orléans was typical of the architecture of New France.

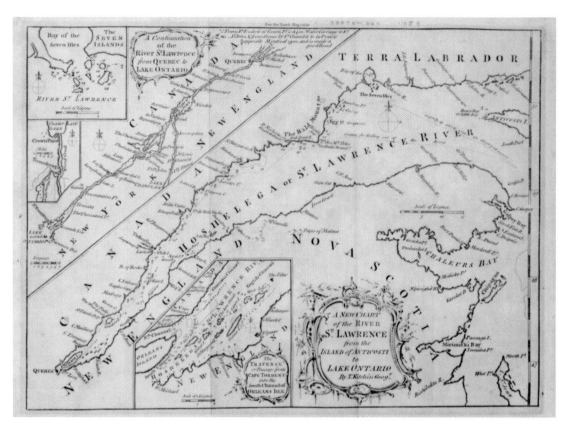

This British map of the St Lawrence River dates from around 1764.

This drawing, made by an unknown artist before 1835, is called "Old Seigneurial Manor House."

Furthermore, they did not think the British would be able to navigate safely past all the river's hazards. But with the help of several kidnapped French pilots and of a young navigator named James Cook who made soundings and charts of the river as the fleet progressed, the British made it to Ile d'Orléans.

The French position was difficult to attack so the British waited for several weeks, meanwhile firing cannonballs at the town from across the river, plundering and burning nearby habitants' farms, and attempting an unsuccessful assault on nearby Beauport. But when summer turned to autumn, the British knew they had to act before the river froze up. Finally they discovered a path up the cliff, just upstream from the fortified town. British Admiral James Wolfe and his men crept up the cliff during the night and attacked at dawn. When the battle was over, both Wolfe and Montcalm had been fatally wounded, and the British were victorious. The British navy was now in control of the river. Quebec fell five days later and Montreal fell to the British the next year without another shot being fired.

When the 1763 Treaty of Paris finally settled the conflict, France ceded all its North American territories east of the Mississippi River to Britain. Other provisions of the treaty saw the fates of several sugar-producing Caribbean Islands, including Guadeloupe, decided. At the time many people in England would have preferred to keep Guadeloupe rather than Canada, but as it turned out, the colony along the St. Lawrence River was turned over to the British.

The Loyalists

In 1774, the British passed the Quebec Act, giving the French Canadians the right to speak French and to practise their Catholic religion. Some of the act's other provisions regarding territory angered the people of Britain's American colonies and a year later, those irritants contributed to the American Revolution. Expecting that the French Canadians would want to throw off the British administration, an American force attacked Montreal and held it over the winter of 1775-76. However, the city's residents showed little interest in joining the rebellion. Another American force, led by Benedict Arnold and later supplemented by Richard Montgomery, laid siege to Quebec City until the arrival of the British fleet forced them to retreat.

When the War of Independence ended in 1783, thousands of people who had been loyal to the British decided to leave the newly established United States and start new lives in the still British colony to the north. Known as Loyalists, they settled in areas that are now in Nova Scotia, New Brunswick, Quebec and

Following the American Revolution, many people who had stayed loyal to the British moved to Canada. En route up the St. Lawrence River they had to camp out overnight.

When they reached the British colony north of the newly established United States, the Loyalist settlers drew lots for land.

This 1841 engraving titled Prescott from Ogdensburg Harbour was done by William Henry Bartlett.

The Loyalist community of Brockville became very wealthy in the 19th century.

Ontario. Many were farmers of Scottish and other European ancestry.

Some of the Loyalists came down the Richelieu River to Sorel and then to Montreal. There, they boarded flat-bottomed boats called *batteaux*. Native people and "half-breeds" (people of mixed European and aboriginal ancestry) manned the sails, oars and poles that were used to push the batteaux upstream, but the settlers had to walk along the portage trails while the crews towed the boats through stretches of white water.

In 1784 many Loyalists settled along the St. Lawrence around present-day Cornwall and Brockville and along the north shore of Lake Ontario. Upon reaching their destination, the settlers drew lots out of a hat for the piece of riverfront land that was to be allotted to them. They then had to clear the forest and build cabins. Times were difficult at first, but eventually the Loyalists built handsome stone or brick homes and established farms. The river continued to be an important transportation route, and when more villages were developed inland, each village had a road down to the water where a dock could be constructed.

In 1791 the area west of Montreal that had been settled by these English-speaking Loyalists was separated from the rest of the primarily French-speaking colony. Cornwall and points upstream were now part of Upper Canada, while the lower St. Lawrence region became known as Lower Canada.

The American side of the river was opened to settlement after 1787, although it was far from other populated areas of New York State and people were in no rush to build there. Ogdensburg, which had been founded in 1749 as a fort and mission, started to attract settlers around 1796, and by 1812 it rivalled Kingston and Prescott as a commercial centre. But in 1807 the

William Johnston, Pirate of the St. Lawrence

This 1840 print is titled "Engagement in the Thousand Islands."

People who make their living on the river in the Thousand Islands are nicknamed river rats, and the most infamous river rat of all is undoubtedly William Johnston, pirate, smuggler, kidnapper, thief, all-around scoundrel and local hero. Born in Lower Canada, he grew up near Kingston, then moved to the United States. During the War of 1812 the British arrested him for spying and helping the Americans. That sparked in him a burning desire to get revenge on the British.

The most famous incident involving Pirate Bill Johnston was the burning of the steamer *Sir Robert Peel*. The time was May 1838, the place was Wellesley Island in the Thousand Islands and the background included political unrest and armed rebellions in both Upper and Lower Canada. Johnson led a band of about 20 armed men – mostly Canadians who planned to hijack the ship for a rebel navy – aboard the *Sir Robert Peel*. They looted the vessel, sent the passengers ashore and set sail, but when they ran aground, they decided to set it on fire.

In November of the same year, a group of Hunters – a secret organization of Americans who wanted to help free Canadians from what they saw as British oppression and install a republic north of the border – decided to invade Canada at Prescott. Johnston piloted one of their three boats. They landed at a stone windmill where they expected Canadian and American reinforcements. Instead, they ran into British soldiers and Canadian militia. During the Battle of the Windmill almost 100 men died, but Johnston escaped.

The Americans arrested Johnston for piracy, but he escaped from jail. He was eventually pardoned and thereafter earned his living as a lighthouse keeper, tavern owner and smuggler. Romantic novels appeared about his exploits, and the burning of the *Sir Robert Peel* was memorialized in song.

This is what the site of the Battle of the Windmill looked like in 1839.

This drawing of the Cascade rapids and lock on the St. Lawrence, southwest of Montreal, dates from about 1820.

This ice bridge at Long Point, near Montreal, was painted in 1860 by civil engineer William H. E. Napier.

Americans passed a law restricting trade between the United States and any British possession, an embargo that damaged the livelihoods of many lumber workers and forced some merchants into smuggling.

In 1812 anger over Britain's policies at sea led the United States to declare war on the British. Fighting took place in Nova Scotia, Detroit and Chateauguay, southwest of Montreal, where the British fought off an invasion attempt. The St. Lawrence River, on the international boundary, once again became a war zone.

The river acted as a critical supply route to Upper Canada since roads were still primitive. But it wasn't easy: the trip from Montreal to Kingston took two weeks, and the river was impassable in winter. Convoys of batteaux, protected by gunboats, made the trip safer from enemy attack.

To protect the river, the British built a blockhouse at Coteau du Lac, west of Montreal, and a garrison at Fort Wellington, near present-day Prescott. The Americans attacked Gananoque in Upper Canada, the British took Ogdensburg. Prisoners were seized, boats scuttled and ambushes laid, but the biggest encounter took place in November 1813 on the riverside farm belonging to Loyalist settler John Crysler, near Morrisburg, Ontario. There, about 800 British troops and local militia fought off an American force more than twice their size. Peace returned in 1814.

Canals, Ships and Bridges

In the 19th century the upper St. Lawrence began to play an important role in commercial trade. Competition for commercial traffic intensified after the Americans built the Erie Canal in 1825 between Lake Ontario and the Hudson River. It was time to construct a new canal system on the upper St. Lawrence.

Grosse Ile –
Island of Tragedy

Grosse Ile, about 50 kilometres (30 miles) downriver from Quebec City, played a tragic role in Canadian history. In 1832, a huge wave of immigrants from the British Isles flooded into Canada, but a cholera epidemic was sweeping Europe, so Canadian authorities established a quarantine station on Grosse Ile. All ships had to stop there, passengers had to be examined by doctors and ships needed health certificates before proceeding to Quebec City.

Between 1845 and 1847 thousands of Irish immigrants, fleeing poverty and famine, left their homeland for Canada. Many died of typhus during the Atlantic crossing, and between 10,000 and 12,000 Irish immigrants are buried on Grosse Ile. The worst outbreak of typhus occurred in 1847, when 20,000 people were treated on the island.

Grosse Ile continued its role as a quarantine station until 1937. Between 1938 and 1957 it was taken over by the military. During World War II, authorities were concerned the Nazis might use biological weapons, so scientists working on the island developed vaccines against diseases such as anthrax. They continued top-secret research on chemical and biological weapons during the 1950's. In 1958 the island was turned over to Canada's Department of Agriculture and was used for research on diseases that affect livestock and as a quarantine station for imported animals. The island is now a National Historic Site.

These immigrants were waiting for a medical exam at Grosse Ile.

Immigrants quarantined on Grosse Ile were housed in various accommodations, including this second-class hotel.

The Irish graveyard on Grosse Ile became the final destination for many unlucky immigrants.

Lightships were anchored near hazardous spots during the navigation season.

This 1872 photo shows the timber coves near Quebec City, where the floating logs were collected before being shipped overseas.

The first canal and lock system in North America had been completed around a stretch of rapids on the St. Lawrence at Coteau du Lac in 1781. In the 19th century more canals were built or enlarged, the most important of which was the Lachine Canal on the island of Montreal, bypassing the Lachine Rapids, first opened in 1825 and enlarged in the 1840's and 1870's. A canal at Beauharnois was completed in 1845. By 1848 the St. Lawrence was equipped with canals from Montreal to Kingston, although boats generally only used the canals on the upstream voyage. On the downstream journey, they took the faster but riskier route through the rapids. During the same period, a vast regional water transportation system was completed with construction of the Welland, Chambly and Rideau Canals. These canals were also an important part of Canada's defences since water transportation was essential for moving supplies.

In the mid-1800's other improvements to navigation on the St. Lawrence were completed. Lighthouse beacons were installed to guide ships to safety. A harbour commission was formed in Montreal in 1830, and stone wharves, walls to protect the waterfront area from flooding and waterfront railroad facilities were constructed. In 1851 the river was dredged for the first time downstream from Montreal, especially through the shallows of Lake St. Pierre.

With these improvements in transportation, and with the provision of hydro power, new industries prospered. Textile factories, tanneries, flour mills, sugar refineries and foundries appeared near the banks of the St. Lawrence River and the Lachine Canal. The fur trade was coming to an end, and these industries fuelled the growth of Montreal. The city was also a transfer point for supplies being forwarded to Upper Canada, and for timber and grain being shipped east from Upper Canada. In 1851, 258 overseas vessels visited the port of Montreal.

This was the age of the river baron, as entrepreneurs made their fortunes from shipping companies and shipyards. For example, Sir Hugh Allan established the Allan Line which transported passengers, general cargo, mail and troops between England and North America, and he invested the money he made in shipping in other businesses, including insurance, banking, mining and manufacturing.

The timber trade was at its peak between 1850 and 1880. Loggers harvested mostly red and white pine as well as some oak and elm. They cut the logs square, tied the timbers together and floated huge rafts down the St. Lawrence from the Great Lakes, or down the Ottawa, and then to the seaport at Quebec. The longest, straightest timbers were destined to become the masts of sailing ships, but most of the timber was shipped to England to be used in construction and carpentry.

The New York side of the river also thrived as a result of logging and shipbuilding. Clayton became a centre for timber raft construction, and a shipyard employing 250 people opened there in the 1830's to produce schooners, skiffs and steam-powered vessels. Alexandria Bay was founded as a lumbering centre and supply station, but by mid-century it had hotels catering to wealthy visitors attracted to the area for sport fishing. In 1850 a railway reached Ogdensburg, and soon a ferry carried railway cars back and forth across the river to Prescott.

In the 19th century the St. Lawrence renewed its role as a main entry point for new immigrants. Around 1815 thousands of people started leaving Great Britain for Canada. Most arrived via Quebec City and Montreal and eventually settled in Upper Canada. Montreal's population increased from 16,000 in 1815 to 58,000 in 1851,

Dozens of masts sprout above Montreal harbour.

At Bic, a three-masted square rigger sailing ship waits for a pilot to guide it on the river.

Steamers replaced sailing ships on Montreal's busy wharves.

The lighthouse at Pointe au Père, near Rimouski, is the one of the tallest in Canada.

The Victoria Bridge was originally built as a tubular train bridge.

while Upper Canada grew from 487,000 people in 1842 to 1.4 million in 1861.

Conditions aboard the crowded immigrant ships were appalling, and many people died during the voyage across the Atlantic. The diseases that plagued the ships also spread on land. There was no such thing as garbage collection, sanitary sewers or water treatment plants, and people did not understand how diseases were transmitted, so devastating cholera, small pox and typhus outbreaks occurred at Montreal and several other port cities.

While water transportation still reigned supreme, rail travel was the transportation method of the future. For Montreal, an island city, this presented a problem. Passengers and freight had to be unloaded and carried across the St. Lawrence on ferries. In 1853 a ferry was built that could transport a locomotive and three rail cars across the river. During the cold winter months the St. Lawrence was put into service as an ice road.

The long-term solution, however, was to build a bridge across the St. Lawrence. Some people thought the scheme was crazy: bridge engineering was in its infancy in the 1850's, the current was strong and a bridge would have to survive thick ice and the extremes of Montreal's climate. In addition, at 2.7 kilometres (1.7 miles), this would be the longest bridge in the world. The bridge took six years to build, between 1,500 and 3,000 men worked on it at any one time and 26 lives were lost during its construction. Finally, when the Prince of Wales came to Canada to open it in 1860, the Victoria Bridge was hailed as the Eighth Wonder of the World. Originally built to handle just one train at a time, the bridge was redesigned in 1897 to accommodate trains, streetcars and automobiles.

Lighthouses of the St. Lawrence

The most hazardous part of the river was between the lower estuary and Quebec City. Fog, gales and late autumn blizzards added to the hazards posed by some 84 islands and islets, unusual currents and underwater shoals. In the period between 1840 and 1849 alone, 233 ships were grounded or wrecked. The government set up several depots supplied with food along the river to help save the lives of shipwrecked mariners.

The first lighthouse on the river, built in 1809, was located on Ile Verte, and it remained the sole lighthouse until 1830. By 1862 there were about 20 lighthouses and lightships between Quebec City and the Strait of Belle Isle. Lightships were anchored near sandbanks and reefs during the shipping season. In the 20th century, lightships were replaced by permanent pillar lights. Beacons were fueled by coal oil (kerosene) or by porpoise and wolf-fish oil.

Although lonely, hazardous and poorly-paid, the job of lightkeeping was considered quite desirable. Lighthouse keepers were well respected in their communities, and the position was often passed on from father to son, brother or cousin. The best positions were in light stations close to communities where the keepers and their families could easily get supplies. Life on isolated islands or pillar stations was harsh, and over the years at least 12 lightkeepers drowned while crossing the river by sailboat to collect fresh drinking water and supplies.

The 20th Century

As the 20th century dawned, the upper stretches of the river and its tributaries were increasingly industrialized and populated. By 1903 the world's second-largest hydroelectric power plant had been constructed on the St. Maurice River. Industries such as a pulp and

The lighthouse at Pointe des Monts, on the lower north shore, marks the end of the estuary and the beginning of the Gulf of St. Lawrence.

The lighthouse on Ile Verte is the oldest on the river.

Permanent pillar lights replaced lightships in the 20th century.

The Empress of Ireland

On a mild, calm day in May 1914, the *Empress of Ireland* cast off from a pier at Quebec City, bound for Liverpool, England, with 1,479 passengers and crew aboard. Passengers included newly married couples, children, members of a Salvation Army band and industrial workers from Detroit returning to Europe to visit relatives.

Late that night the Canadian Pacific liner was off Pointe au Père (Father Point), near Rimouski, when a patch of fog wrapped itself around the ship. Through the gloom, the officer on duty spotted the lights of another vessel. A few minutes later the *Storstad*, a Norwegian cargo ship carrying 10,000 tons of coal, sliced into the starboard side of the liner.

The *Empress* quickly began to fill with water and rolled onto her side. Passengers grabbed their life belts, but the deck was on such a steep angle that some of them fell into the frigid river. The *Empress of Ireland* sank within 15 minutes of the collision, and 1,012 people died. Those who survived clung to debris or managed to get into lifeboats and were taken on board the *Storstad* or one of two other vessels that rushed to the scene to help, while one man managed to swim to shore.

Today divers visit the liner's underwater grave, and an exhibit at Pointe au Père is dedicated to the memory of those who died in Canada's worst maritime disaster.

paper plants and chemical factories were soon taking advantage of the cheap electricity, abundant labour and natural resources available in the region.

Meanwhile, the St. Lawrence corridor was no longer the only option for local transportation. Rail had replaced water as the preferred method of transporting many goods and passengers, and roads were improving. But the river was increasingly busy with international shipping since it provided the shortest route between central North America and Europe. Montreal became an important port for cargo vessels from Europe and around the world. As the century progressed, port facilities were constantly modernized and navigational aids were improved.

By mid-century it had become clear that a modern canal system was needed so large vessels could travel between Montreal and the Great Lakes. In 1951 the Canadian government set up the St. Lawrence Seaway Authority with a mandate to construct, maintain and operate the Seaway, either wholly in Canada or in partnership with the United States. In 1954 the American government set up an agency to build a portion of the Seaway on the U.S. side of the river. The discovery of large iron ore deposits in northeastern Quebec and Labrador encouraged development of the Seaway to transport the ore to industrial cities around the Great Lakes.

Construction of the St. Lawrence section of the Seaway was a monumental task that took five years. The project included building canals, locks and dams, deepening the riverbed and flooding large areas. Before Lake St. Lawrence was flooded, a major highway and forty miles of railway tracks had to be moved. Seven small villages (still remembered today as the lost villages) disappeared under the water and were replaced by two brand new towns, Long Sault and Ingleside. Parts of two other towns were also relocated. In all, about 6,500 people were affected, and 550 dwellings were pulled to new locations by huge house-moving machines. Land around the new lake was set aside for wildlife sanctuaries, parks and tourist attractions. The Seaway officially opened in 1959.

Until the early 1960's, the navigation season on the St. Lawrence usually lasted from April to December, but Montreal needed to compete with ports along the eastern seaboard that were open year-round. Also, ice accumulation frequently caused destructive floods. In 1962 Canadian Coast Guard icebreakers began keeping the channel open as far upstream as Montreal. The *Helga Dan*, a Danish merchant ship, sailed into history on January 4, 1964, when she became the first ship to reach Montreal in the month of January. That signalled the beginning of the St. Lawrence's career as a year-round navigable waterway.

Another revolution in shipping practices occurred when the port of Montreal's first container terminal opened in 1968. Prior to the advent of containers, it could take several weeks to unload and load a ship's cargo, and the port employed some 3,000 dockworkers. Containers reduced turn-around times to a few days, and the work was done by large cranes rather than by manual labourers.

Since then, port facilities and navigational aids along the river have been modernized and expanded, and the shipping channel has been deepened so that ever-larger ships can reach Montreal. Governments and citizens have also turned their attention to cleaning up the environment and protecting the St. Lawrence's natural beauty and wildlife.

The Soulanges Canal was completed in 1899 on the north shore of the St. Lawrence between Lake St. Louis and Lake St. François. It provided a detour for boats around the Coteau, Cedar and Split Rock Rapids and replaced several earlier canals. It was closed in 1959 when the St. Lawrence Seaway opened.

This 1903 photo shows that the Lachine Canal was an industrial hub.

The opening of the St. Lawrence Seaway in 1959 was a momentous occasion.

St. Lawrence River skiffs were put to many uses in the Thousand Islands.

The *Rapids King* rides the rapids near Cornwall.

A rowboat was handy for checking on the fields during the spring floods.

This sketch of a Durham Boat on the St. Lawrence was done about 1832.

Schooners were the workhorses of the St. Lawrence estuary.

These unidentified people were going out for a sail on the river.

Boats and Ships of the St. Lawrence

Besides being a source of furs and fish, the St. Lawrence also provided access to another plentiful resource: big, strong timbers, perfect for building ships. A homegrown shipbuilding industry started at Quebec in the 1660's. Commercial vessels, navy ships, fishing boats and other vessels were all produced at shipyards along the river and in the Great Lakes. The biggest boom in shipbuilding coincided with an increase in the market for timber at the beginning of the 19th century. Some ships were built and sailed to England, then immediately taken apart so the timber could be sold. The height of Canadian shipbuilding lasted from 1849 to 1895.

During World War I shipyards along the St. Lawrence were very busy manufacturing steel barges and other vessels for the war effort. More than 15,000 people worked at the Vickers Company shipyard in Montreal, while other shipyards also went into high gear. Shipyards on the St. Lawrence worked even harder during World War II to produce mine sweepers, frigates, corvettes, trawlers and other vessels.

After 1945 the ship-building and repair industries on the St. Lawrence went into gradual decline, although naval frigates, ferries, ice-breakers, hovercraft and oil drilling platforms were produced in the second half of 20th century.

Over this 400-year period, various types of boats and ships have come and gone on the St. Lawrence. The first vessels were canoes made by the native people. Covered with bark and sealed with spruce gum, the canoes were lightweight, fast, and easy to manoeuvre and carry over portages. They were about five metres (16 feet) long. The fur-traders copied the original design, but enlarged them to carry more men and supplies. The Montreal canoe, for example, was 11

Shipyards along the banks of the St. Lawrence were in high gear during World War II. Here, a workman examines a ship's propeller while surrounded by parts used in the assembly of merchant freighters in a Montreal shipyard.

This ship, docked near Montreal, became encrusted with ice as it made its way up the river. Winter navigation became possible on the St. Lawrence in 1964.

An octagonal blockhouse, or fort, was built at Coteau du Lac at the outbreak of the War of 1812 to protect this strategically important spot on the transportation corridor between Upper and Lower Canada.

The Fleming Mill, overlooking the St. Lawrence in the LaSalle borough of Montreal, was constructed in 1827. It is the only remaining mill in Quebec to have been constructed in an Anglo-Saxon architectural style.

The Lachine Canal was built in 1825 to connect Lake St. Louis and Montreal harbour. Today, located next to the canal and in a warehouse once used to store furs and trade goods, is The Fur Trade at Lachine National Historic Site, a museum devoted to the fur trade.

metres (36 feet) long and able to carry up to four tons of people, furs and supplies.

On the upper St. Lawrence, long, narrow, open-decked batteaux and Durham boats transported goods and people between Montreal and Kingston. Batteaux were constructed of wood (often cedar) and had flat bottoms so they wouldn't get stuck in shallow water. The French had used small batteaux in the 1700's to transport military supplies, but later models were about 20 metres (65 feet) long. Durham boats, similar to the barges used on American canals, appeared at the beginning of the 19th century. Driven by sails, poled through shallow water, or pulled by teams of oxen and horses on the shore, they were longer and wider than batteaux and could carry 12 to 14 tons of passengers and goods. By 1835, an estimated 1,500 batteaux and 500 Durham boats operated above Montreal.

A variety of sailboats plied the river for more than two centuries. Between 1700 and 1850, the most spectacular were the three-masted square-riggers. The largest of these were between 200 and 1,000 tons, and were used to carry trade goods across the Atlantic. Two-masted brigantines were also a common sight. Square-sailed, they varied between 60 and 150 tons. Large brigantines crossed the ocean, while smaller ones were used for coastal trade with the United States and the Caribbean. The 1700's and early 1800's were known as the golden age of sail.

The age of steam began with great excitement on the St. Lawrence in 1809, when the first steamship appeared on the Quebec City-Montreal run. It was built in Montreal by brewer and banker John Molson. The *Accommodation* had two side paddlewheels, as well as sails – in case the engine failed. Within a few years several steamship companies were competing for freight and passengers on this busy stretch of river. The steamers began racing each other to see which would be the first to reach its destination, and the crews did whatever they could, no matter how foolhardy, to heat up their boilers and increase speed. One such race turned to tragedy in 1857 when the steamer *Montreal* caught fire and ran aground, killing 253 people. There were no more races after that.

On the upper St. Lawrence, small side-wheel steamers plied back and forth between the sections of rapids. Flat-bottomed, wooden-hulled craft, they had wood-burning boilers. In 1842 British author Charles Dickens described his voyage from Kingston to Montreal, alternating between steamboat and stage-coach. Later, large steamboats shot the rapids, expertly guided by legendary pilots like Big John from the nearby Mohawk reserve.

In the late 19th century a type of rowboat called the St. Lawrence River skiff was the best way to get around the Thousand Islands region. About five metres (16 feet) long, narrow, light and stable, these skiffs were very fast. People also sailed them, but there was no rudder, so they steered by shifting their weight, just like sailboarders manoeuvre their craft today. The first skiff was probably made in Clayton, but boat builders on both sides of the river constructed them.

In the first half of the 20th century, the gleaming white ships of Canada Steamship Lines' (CSL) Great White Fleet were a familiar sight on the St. Lawrence each summer. These passenger vessels travelled the St. Lawrence system in relays, since conditions on different parts of the river required different types of boat construction. One fleet was designed to cruise the Great Lakes. A second fleet of paddle wheelers took passengers from Toronto through the Thousand Islands to Prescott. At Prescott, passengers boarded vessels designed to shoot the rapids at Long Sault and Lachine. It was a wild

Arctic Explorer

Of all the mariners the St. Lawrence River has produced, the most celebrated was Joseph Elzéar Bernier. Born in 1852 in the tiny community of l'Islet, near Ile d'Orléans, he came from a family of mariners. At age 14, he dropped out of school to work as a cabin boy; three years later he was the captain of a brigantine carrying timber to Britain. During his career he commanded 105 ships and crossed the Atlantic Ocean 269 times. But Bernier's most important contribution was as captain of the steamer *Arctic*, which patrolled the northern waters in the early 1900's. As an explorer, he charted previously unknown areas and established Canadian sovereignty by claiming the Arctic islands for Canada. He died at Lévis in 1934.

Captain Joseph-Elzear Bernier, C.G.S., Arctic Expedition, 1923.

The Battle of the Windmill National Historic Site is located near Prescott, Ontario. Although originally a windmill, this building was at one time converted into a lighthouse.

ride, dodging submerged rocks, and white spray flew into the passengers' faces. The last CSL passenger boat to make the trip was the *Rapids Prince* in 1949. Another part of the fleet sailed from Montreal, taking passengers to the hotels and cottages of Murray Bay and the Saguenay fjord. Like today's cruise ships, these vessels provided guests with luxurious accommodations, good food and entertainment, as well as beautiful scenery.

Schooners, known in French as *goélettes,* were the workhorses of the lower St. Lawrence. These two-masted vessels transported passengers and supplies to communities along the estuary, carrying everything from pulpwood to potatoes. Schooners were built at small shipyards around the estuary, and their captains and crews were usually people who had grown up on the river. The first motor-driven schooner chugged down the St. Lawrence in 1934, and metal-hulled schooners carried heavy machinery to the lower north shore around 1970. Soon after that, trucks and improved highways made these vessels obsolete.

U-Boats in the St. Lawrence

Late in the evening of May 11, 1942, the opening shot was fired in what would become the Battle of the St. Lawrence. That night a German U-boat torpedoed a British merchant ship carrying war supplies to Great Britain and sank her. Two hours later the same submarine sank a Dutch freighter.

The Battle of the St. Lawrence lasted from May 1942 to November 1944. In all, 15 German U-boats prowled the waters of the gulf and sailed as far upriver as Rimouski, about 300 kilometres (185 miles) downstream from Quebec City. They attacked 29 vessels, including merchant ships, warships that were escorting the merchant marine convoys, an American troop ship and a domestic ferry crossing the gulf. All but three of the torpedoed ships exploded, burned and sank, with the loss of hundreds of lives.

Guns were installed on the shore near Quebec City and aircraft patrolled the river, but the Royal Canadian Navy was hampered by inadequately trained crews on its vessels, a lack of advanced sonar and radar equipment, and poor communications along the shores of the St. Lawrence. The river itself presented another difficulty as layers of water at different temperatures and levels of salinity helped to hide the submarines.

This monument, located on the waterfront in Quebec City, is dedicated to the sailors from Quebec who joined Canada's merchant marine fleet and died at sea during World War II. The monument was unveiled in 2002.

CHAPTER THREE

Flora and Fauna

When explorer Jacques Cartier sailed up the St. Lawrence in 1535, he was amazed to see so many whales, porpoises and walruses. Today, the walruses are long gone and others species, such as the beluga whale, are endangered. Years of over-fishing, pollution, dredging of the river bottom and land-filling of the shoreline have all contributed to the damage done to the environment.

However, numerous healthy wildlife habitats remain. The jewels that crown this majestic river include wetlands for nesting and spawning, broad intertidal flats and underwater currents, swirling with nutrients. In the estuary, whales break the surface, their backs gleaming. Great blue herons wade in shallow marshes and tidal flats, while snow geese fill the sky during their spring and fall migrations. Muskellunge, known as the king of sport fish, lurk among freshwater shoals, and schools of tiny capelin and shrimp provide feasts for hungry fish and seabirds in the estuary and gulf.

Snow geese flock to Cap Tourmente, near Quebec City, during their autumn migration.

The wetlands at Cooper Marsh begin to turn from winter brown to spring green in early May.

The Lachine Rapids are a unique, unspoiled treasure just upstream from the bustling port of Montreal.

The St. Lawrence River is home to 185 salt-water and fresh-water species of fish. There are at least 17 species of amphibians (mostly frogs and salamanders) and 16 species of reptiles, primarily snakes and turtles, between Cornwall and Anticosti Island. More than 18 species of ducks and geese either nest on the river or stop to feed there during migration. Smaller birds, such as sandpipers, swallows and sparrows, spend their summers along the river, although most species migrate south in winter. Nine species of whales and dolphins are regular visitors to the estuary.

The complex combinations of conditions created by tides, currents, channel depth, salt content, temperature, climate and bottom material create a huge variety of aquatic and shore-line habitats for plants and wildlife. Meanwhile, human activities have made a great impact on the river, changing it forever.

The Fluvial Section: People and Wetlands

The Thousand Islands encompass many unique environments because they are at a point where several different climates and types of forests intersect. The balsam firs and ground cedars found there are typical of the boreal forests to the north, while black and silver maples are normally found in more southern forests. These islands have acidic soil like the Canadian Shield to the north, but nearby Lake Ontario acts to keep winters mild. Some of the islands have unique local climate conditions due to combinations of landscape, wind and water.

Because they offer such varied habitats, the Thousand Islands provide shelter for many animals. The cougars, wolves, moose and black bears that used to roam the area have disappeared, but red fox, flying squirrels, mink and white-tailed deer still thrive there. The islands have the largest numbers of species of amphib-

This is a typical scene in the Thousand Islands.

Hardy conifers and birches survive in the harsh climate of north shore Les Escoumins, downriver from Tadoussac.

A variety of plants thrive in the wetlands of the Cooper Marsh conservation area near Cornwall, Ontario.

A black-crowned night heron rests near the Lachine Rapids.

ians and reptiles in Canada, including harmless black rat snakes, the largest snake in Canada at up to 2.5 metres (eight feet) in length, as well as northern water snakes and chatty spring peepers. In the swift-flowing channels, underwater shoals and quiet bays between the islands, the area is home to 88 species of fish.

Downstream from the Thousand Islands, the river is popular with sports fishermen in search of walleye, northern pike and smallmouth bass. Common species of terrestrial animals along the fluvial section and its many tributaries include the northern leopard frog, snapping turtle, common garter snake, ring-billed gull (which has become something of a pest around city dumps), muskrat and beaver. Red or white trilliums, white anemones and delicate violets decorate the forest floor in early spring, Queen

Anne's lace and orange hawkweed sway in summer breezes, and sunny meadows are sprinkled with tall goldenrod and tiny purple asters in autumn.

Just around the Montreal area, more than 20 species of amphibians and reptiles and 250 bird species can be found. Thousands of songbirds and waterfowl nest here or migrate through the area, stopping to rest and feed on the river or in city parks and suburban gardens. Minutes from downtown Montreal is a small stretch of truly wild river, the Lachine Rapids, where the St. Lawrence races around submerged rocks and through deep pools at a speed of up to four metres (13 feet) per second. Some 50 species of fish live in and around the rapids and 28 species breed there, including rainbow trout and brown trout which spawn in the fast current, while

In the Lake St. Pierre archipelago near Sorel, agricultural and recreational uses, as well as alien plants species such as purple loosestrife, create stresses on the environment.

Pointe du Buisson was an excellent fishing spot for generations of aboriginal people. Today it is a beautiful place to watch the river go by.

smallmouth bass, muskellunge and northern pike prefer sheltered spots.

Although the freshwater fluvial section is the most heavily populated and developed part of the river, it also contains 80 per cent of the St. Lawrence River's wetlands. Wetlands help to keep the river healthy, functioning like its lungs and kidneys, as the microscopic organisms that live there filter and purify the water and recycle organic matter. Submerged and floating plants and marsh species such as bulrushes, willows and other shrubs act to slow wave action and currents, thereby decreasing shoreline erosion. Wetlands also provide homes for insects, birds, amphibians, reptiles and aquatic mammals, such as muskrat.

Some of the largest areas of marshes and wet meadows are on the shores and islands of Lake St. Pierre. In April and May flood waters cover almost twice its normal area. Normally an average three metres (9.8 feet) deep, the water level rises an average 1.3 metres (4.3 feet), and sometimes as much as 3.6 metres (11.8 feet). The flooded area offers an ideal environment for migrating and nesting ducks, for spawning fish such as the northern pike and yellow perch, and for breeding amphibians. As the spring sun warms the lake, small organisms including plankton, insects, worms, crustaceans and mollusks proliferate, providing food for larger creatures. When the flood waters recede, their remains leave the farmland naturally fertilized.

Despite their importance, however, an estimated two-thirds of the wetlands of the lower Great Lakes and St. Lawrence River have disappeared over the last 400 years. Humans are to blame when they build roads, houses, industries, port or recreational facilities, when farmers or developers fill in marshes to use the land, or when waves created by large ships disturb wetlands.

A great blue heron waits patiently for something to eat. This individual nests on an island in the Lachine Rapids.

The Great Blue Heron

The great blue heron, stalking through shallow water, watching for a small fish or frog for lunch, is a common sight along the St. Lawrence. There are more than 35 nesting colonies along the river, especially on islands that are safe from predators and people. In fact, one of the largest great blue heron colonies in North America, with more than 1,000 nesting pairs of birds, is on Grande Ile in Lake St. Pierre. There are also large colonies of great blue herons and of black-crowned night herons on a protected island site in the middle of the Lachine Rapids. Environmental pressures on these birds include disappearing habitats, disturbances by humans during nesting season, illegal hunting and eggs contaminated by low levels of toxic chemicals.

Wetlands of the Estuary

Between Lake St. Pierre and Quebec City steep banks envelop the river, and there are few natural wetlands. But downstream from Quebec City both the north and south shores are rich in wetlands, although they are quite different from the wetlands of the fluvial St. Lawrence. For one thing, the shore is regularly flooded at high tide. Also, the brackish water limits the growth of both fresh and salt-water species of plants and animals: it's too salty for the freshwater species, and not salty enough for marine species. But vast expanses of American bulrushes (*Scirpus americanus*) thrive in these conditions, so these wetlands are called scirpus marshes.

Although the number of species of birds found here is limited, there are lots of individuals of a few species. The scirpus marsh at Cap Tourmente, east of Quebec City, is a favourite spot for the greater snow goose, especially during the fall migration, since bulrush roots are among their favourite foods. Other birds that frequent the river in this area include teals, pintails and black ducks.

Common fish found in these brackish waters include smelts, yellow perch, brown bullhead, American eel and Atlantic tomcod. Some species are diadromous, meaning they can live in both salt and fresh water, although they generally do so at different times in their life cycles. For example, Atlantic sturgeon and American shad fish live most of their lives in salt water but breed in fresh, while American eels live in fresh water and breed at sea.

The breeding habits of the Atlantic tomcod inspire an annual ritual in Quebec. The tomcod come in vast numbers to the mouth of the St. Anne River, west of Quebec City, each January to spawn. People drag huts onto the ice and sit comfortably inside the warmed huts while they fish through holes in the ice. Meanwhile, the

Marsh marigolds appear in moist areas of the St. Lawrence River valley in late spring.

Yellow pond lilies decorate quiet streams throughout the St. Lawrence River drainage basin.

Snow geese put their heads right down into the mud to get at the roots of the scirpus bulrushes.

Too Many Geese

To bird lovers, the sight of hundreds of thousands of migrating greater snow geese on the banks of the St. Lawrence each spring and fall is awesome. But in recent years, these geese have become too numerous for their own good. More than 950,000 birds are destroying the riverside farm crops they rely on and upsetting the natural balance of the marshes where they feed. In response, the government introduced a spring conservation hunt in 1999 to try to control the greater snow goose population.

Freshwater Fish

Here are a few of the approximately 100 freshwater fish species found in the St. Lawrence and its tributaries:

Common throughout Canada and abundant  in the lakes of the St. Lawrence, the **yellow perch** is popular with anglers. Yellow perch travel in schools, preying on invertebrates and small fish. They have two dorsal fins, one of which is spiny, and greenish backs and yellow sides with dark, vertical stripes. Spawning in lake shallows or streams, they lay long strings of gelatinous eggs that float on the current until they get caught on vegetation or on the bottom.

The **copper redhorse** is the only fish unique  to Quebec. At one time it is thought to have been quite common, but as a result of pollution and loss of habitat, it is now a threatened species, despite efforts to increase its population on the Richelieu River. Individuals have a 20-year life span and do not reach sexual maturity until age 10. This coppery-coloured fish has a small head, and its strong teeth are located behind, rather than in, its mouth, an adaptation for crushing mollusk shells.

The **bowfin**, also called the dogfish, can be  identified by the single long fin on its back, its olive colour and stout shape. This species is the sole survivor of a primitive family of fish otherwise known only through fossils. They feed on crustaceans, insects, larvae and small fish. As well as gills, they have an air bladder that allows them to survive in stagnant or polluted water with low oxygen levels.

Pumpkinseeds are small, bright orange  sunfish that can survive in the cold waters of Canada, including the St. Lawrence and its tributaries, where they feed primarily on snails and other invertebrates. When pumpkinseeds spawn in late spring, the males build and protect the nests.

Once fished commercially, **lake sturgeon**  have declined dramatically, although there is still a relatively large population in Lake St. Lawrence. These fish are very sensitive to changes in habitat and poor water quality. Lake sturgeon are the largest of the river's freshwater species, reaching up to 1.5 metres (five feet) in length and weighing up to 30 kilograms (66 pounds). These are very primitive fish, with skeletons of cartilage rather than bone, and rows of armour-like plates on their bodies. They use sensitive barbels to find food on the river bottom, and have a long mouth to suck up plants and animals.

tomcod lay their eggs on the frazil, or ice granules that form a kind of slush on the water's surface. Surrounded and protected by the ice crystals, the eggs are carried downstream in spring to the brackish waters near Ile aux Grues, where the juvenile fish grow to adulthood.

From Kamouraska through the lower estuary, *Spartina alterniflora*, or salt-water cord grass, and other salt-tolerant plants grow in riverside marshes. Spartina salt marshes are rich ecosystems, capable of producing three times more plant matter than a well-fertilized cornfield of the same size, but they are rare: only a few large spartina marshes remain. Low tide in the lower estuary also exposes mud flats and rocks covered with rockweed.

A Marine Environment

The lower estuary and the gulf are both marine environments. Much of the coastline is flat and either rocky or sandy, and there are many small islands and river deltas. In the lower estuary, wetlands are found around lagoons, sandbars and river mouths where the bottom is covered with a mixture of sand, mud and eelgrass. Many varieties of salt-tolerant grasses grow above the high-tide line. Seabirds and wading shorebirds such as gannets and plovers thrive in these surroundings, and herring and plaice spawn in the St. Lawrence. The region is also a breeding ground for mollusks, such as mussels and clams, and for crustaceans like lobsters and rock crabs.

The area around the mouth of the Saguenay, where cold water rising up from the bottom brings nutrients to the surface, is particularly rich in marine life. These nutrients provide food for small invertebrates which, in turn, attract larger creatures. Animals that frequent the waters of the lower estuary and gulf include plankton, such as copepods and krill (tiny

Beside the spartina salt marsh at Isle Verte on the south shore of the estuary, a dike protects agricultural land from the salt water.

Mallard ducks are very common along the St. Lawrence. These females were searching for food in a small stream on the island of Montreal.

Nets are set out in the intertidal zone along the south shore during the autumn eel fishing season.

The Life Cycle of the American Eel

The American eel is not a pretty sight: snakelike and slimy, with a single continuous dorsal and ventral fin, it doesn't inspire even the most passionate nature lovers. Nevertheless, this commercially fished species is in trouble, and scientists are not sure why.

American eels spawn in the Sargasso Sea, an area of warm water in the middle of the Atlantic. The eel larvae drift on the Gulf Stream current toward North America, then metamorphose until they resemble small adult eels. Now called elvers, they migrate up rivers all along the Atlantic seaboard. Only female eels are found in the St. Lawrence River.

The trip up the St. Lawrence takes at least four years. Some stay in the river, and others swim up tributaries, where they remain until they become sexually mature at age 10 to 12. Then the adult females migrate downstream to meet the males in the Sargasso Sea and breed.

As the mature eels make their way toward the sea, eel fishers catch them in weirs: funnel-shaped nets hung on poles stuck in the intertidal mud. Although unpopular in North America, eels bring good prices in Europe and Japan. Until recent years there were hundreds of eel fishermen on the estuary, but the number of eels has declined dramatically, and only a handful of individuals still bother to set up their nets.

A number of factors could be causing this decline, including changes in ocean currents or other factors at sea, disturbances to eel habitats in the river or in Lake Ontario, over-fishing or contamination. Researchers are studying the eels at different stages in their life cycle to find out what is causing the drop in numbers, and to predict their future prospects.

Gertrude Madore, who still sets out her own eel traps every year, runs a museum in Kamouraska dedicated to the eel fishery. Here she demonstrates a model eel trap.

Harbour seals warm themselves on a rock in the lower estuary.

Sea anemones are abundant in this part of the river.

shrimp-like creatures), and bottom-dwelling invertebrates like whelks, periwinkles, barnacles, anemones and sea urchins. Schools of small fish such as herring and capelin feed and spawn here, while halibut, sole, sculpin and Atlantic wolf fish live near the bottom and in the deep, dark waters of the Laurentian Channel.

Marine mammals, including harbour seals and grey seals, also live in this part of the estuary. Fin whales, humpback whales, small minke whales and, occasionally, massive blue whales are regular summer visitors to these nutrient-rich cold waters. These species all have baleen plates in their mouths to filter small fish and crustaceans from the water. Toothed cetaceans found here include beluga whales, Atlantic white-sided dolphins and harbour porpoises.

Diverse marine invertebrate animals in the lower estuary resemble an underwater garden.

If any one creature has come to symbolize the St. Lawrence River, it is probably the beluga. These peaceful whales, with their melon-shaped heads and ghostlike colouration, live in the St. Lawrence and the Saguenay, feeding on a variety of small fish and crustaceans. They are playful and social, swimming together in small groups. Belugas can make about 200 different sounds by passing air through passages in their heads and are the only whales that can turn their heads independently of their bodies.

But many belugas develop tumors and ulcers, and scientists who examine the bodies of dead belugas found washed up on shore think they may die from toxins they ingest. While other species of whales spend only a few months a year in this area, the belugas live here year-round and are exposed to contaminants in the food chain from the time they are calves fed on their mothers' milk.

Belugas were hunted for oil, hides and meat for many decades. The hunt was particularly intense in the 18th and 19th centuries. During the 1930's the Quebec government paid people for killing belugas because commercial fishermen thought they consumed too many fish. In the 1960's construction of hydroelectric dams changed the flow of several tributaries, and this may have affected beluga habitats in the St. Lawrence. It was not until 1973 that researchers started studying these whales. Hunting, chasing or disturbing belugas became illegal in 1980, and the population was declared endangered in 1983. They are now included on Canada's official list of wildlife species at risk and are protected by federal law.

Research scientists can identify each beluga by individual characteristics such as scars. This one is known as Pascolio.

This beluga whale is making a dive.

Researchers now think the St. Lawrence beluga population is stable at about 1,000 to 1,200 individuals. Industrial pollutants entering the river have decreased in recent years, boaters are encouraged not to disturb the whales, a national marine park was established to help protect their habitat, and wildlife groups educate people about them, but their future remains uncertain.

Pollution Problems

Flowing as it does through a populated and industrialized region, the St. Lawrence River has been heavily affected by human activities. Residential and industrial wastes bring bacteria and toxic chemicals, while motor boaters can disturb nesting birds, and construction along the riverbank destroys habitats.

Sediment contamination, especially in the Montreal and Quebec City areas, poses long-term problems since some toxins can accumulate in animal tissues, causing disease or entering the food chain. Several hot-spots in Lake St. Louis and Lake St. Pierre contain enough cadmium, lead, chromium and zinc to have minor effects on bottom-dwelling organisms. Mercury, which is toxic to both fish and humans, occurs naturally in the environment and has also been introduced into the river through industrial and municipal wastes. Walleye and northern pike caught in several areas, especially around Montreal, have high levels of mercury, and the government warns people to eat limited amounts of several fish species.

Large industries have left high levels of PCBs and other contaminants in the sediment, especially downstream from the Moses-Saunders dam at Massena. PCBs, which can cause liver damage and reproductive problems in fish and serious health problems in humans, accumulate in fatty tissues. Lake sturgeon and eels usually have higher levels of PCB contamination than walleye and pike because they have more fat.

Farm wastes also cause environmental problems in the St. Lawrence. Pesticides, used to kill insects, weeds and fungi, but which can also be harmful to fish, run into the river during the spring run-off. Agricultural fertilizers also wash into tributaries, and the nutrients they contain cause algae and other aquatic plants to multiply. When these plants die and decompose, they rob oxygen from the river and make it less attractive to wildlife. Other types of organic matter, such as manure from farm animals, and waste from food processing plants and pulp and paper manufacturing, have the same effect.

The St. Lawrence Seaway and other development projects (most of which were conceived and constructed in the days before environmental impact studies were required) have had a huge impact on the fluvial section of the river. When the Beauharnois power station was built in the 1930's, for example, 84 per cent of the river's flow was diverted to meet its requirement for water, and three stretches of natural rapids disappeared. In other areas, dredging and land-filling disturbed the bottom, and marshes and wetland areas were filled in when roads and dams were built.

Fish habitats also changed drastically after the Seaway opened. The strong current in the deep shipping channel acts like a barrier so fish that inhabit one side of the river don't cross to the other shore. The presence of the Moses-Saunders dam also affected migratory fish, although an eel ladder was built in 1974 to permit these creatures to travel past the obstruction.

In port areas bottom sediments have been contaminated by years of shipping and industrial activity. Other environmental problems asso-

Gannets nest on the rocky shores of the gulf and lower estuary.

A fin whale surfaces near Tadoussac. The average fin whale, a type of baleen whale, is about 20 metres (70 feet) long. In Quebec the fin whale is called *rorqual commun*.

Industries and shipping contribute to pollution on the St. Lawrence.

ciated with harbour activities include the loss of wildlife habitats to wharf construction, and contamination of the water by chemicals used to clean and paint ships.

The shipping channel below Montreal has been deepened and widened almost a dozen times since 1851 so that ever-larger ships could reach the port. Environmental organizations have questioned the wisdom of dredging, suggesting that it disturbs sediments and leaves toxins suspended in the water. Furthermore, larger ships are more destructive because they create bigger waves and cause more shoreline erosion. Passing ships can also harm fish populations when, for example, fish swimming in the shipping channel are sucked into propellers. Increased shipping also brings with it the dangers of collisions and of oil spills.

Gentilly 2, Hydro-Québec's 675-megawatt nuclear generating station, is another potential source of pollution should an accident ever happen there. The aging station has been in operation since 1983.

Shoreline erosion is a problem, especially between Montreal and Lake St. Pierre, where scientists believe that two-thirds of the riverbank is affected. In some places the shoreline has retreated by several metres. What happens is that repeated cycles of freezing and thawing weaken and fracture the riverbanks in winter. During summer, water levels drop and the banks become even more vulnerable when the sun dries them. Then rain and waves caused by storms or passing ships wash the banks away. As a consequence, large quantities of fine marine clay particles are swept downriver, transporting contaminants with them, silting up channels, covering fish spawning grounds and leaving the river less attractive.

Invasive species of plants and animals are another concern. Scientists estimate that some 85 alien species have been introduced into the St. Lawrence during the past two centuries. Once introduced, they tend to move both downstream and upstream and to compete with native species to a lesser or greater extent.

Exotic plants that have invaded the shores of the St. Lawrence drainage area include pretty purple loosestrife and the common reed, both of which can be seen waving in roadside ditches and marshes throughout the region. The most problematic aquatic animal is the zebra mussel, a small but highly prolific mollusk with distinctive brown stripes. The first zebra mussels arrived from Europe in 1986, accidentally introduced in discharged ballast water into the Great Lakes. They have become serious pests there, reaching densities of up to 300,000 mussels per square metre (11 square feet) in some places, clinging to all sorts of underwater surfaces, corroding ships' hulls, blocking water intake pipes and cutting bare feet.

Zebra mussels are found in the fluvial section of the St. Lawrence and in some of its canals and tributaries, but the salinity of the river below Ile d'Orléans near Quebec City prevents them from expanding further into the estuary. Nor have their numbers reached the proportions found in the Great Lakes since, at their floating larval stage, many are swept downstream to their deaths in the salty estuary. Nevertheless, they have changed the ecological balance of the river, consuming all the phytoplankton at the bottom of the food chain so that the minnows and newly hatched fish that depend on these creatures starve. With the disappearance of the plankton that gave the fluvial St. Lawrence its distinctive

Sailboats moored on Lake St. Louis await their owners on a weekday afternoon.

The shoreline along Ile des Soeurs (Nun's Island), a few minutes from downtown Montreal, appears relatively clean. An estimated 49 million cars cross the nearby Champlain Bridge every year.

The shores of the Montreal archipelago are busy places.

Heavy industries, such as oil refineries, are common at the east end of Montreal Island.

green hue, the water is crystal clear but depleted of life.

Another newcomer that has biologists worried is the round goby, a small but aggressive fish from the Caspian Sea. Round gobies eat small minnows and the eggs and young of other species, and biologists are concerned that they will take over the habitats of local fish.

Good News

In recent years most of the news about the quality of water in the St. Lawrence has been good. Despite continuing concerns about water quality, wetlands and certain wildlife species, according to scientists at Environment Canada's St. Lawrence Centre research facility in Montreal, the overall outlook is positive. Contamination from toxic substances has de-

creased and some animal populations have been re-established. Freshwater fish populations remain diverse, the river still has large areas of healthy wetlands and many types of freshwater fish and marine organisms are fit for human consumption.

Although most Quebec municipalities did not begin treating their sewage until the late 1970's through the mid 1990's, and even now only primary treatment is provided, most people who live along the freshwater sections of the St. Lawrence, including 40 per cent of Quebecers, get their drinking water from the river. In fact, intakes are in fast-flowing spots where the water has always been relatively clean. Another good sign is that some riverside beaches that were closed to swimming for years are now open. However, waste from storm sewers and farm manure continues to contribute bacteria to the St. Lawrence and its tributaries.

Efforts to clean up the Great Lakes and St. Lawrence River include agreements between industries and governments in Canada and the United States, such as the Great Lakes Water Quality Agreement. State, provincial and national environmental protection laws and regulations help protect the river, and port authorities and coast guard services are prepared to deal with accidents and spills. Meanwhile dozens of citizens' organizations and aboriginal people in the United States and Canada are helping to protect the St. Lawrence.

As the sole outlet of the Great Lakes, the St. Lawrence also plays an important role in restoring the ecological health of the lakes. Dams near Cornwall, Long Sault and Iroquois, Ontario, are used to manage water levels on the Great Lakes, as well as to ensure there is enough water in the river to generate hydroelectricity and to permit commercial navigation.

In 1988 the governments of Canada and Quebec launched a joint program to clean up the St. Lawrence and reclaim it for use by the public. One measure involved identifying industrial plants that release waste water into the river and its tributaries. These plants, primarily in the pulp and paper, inorganic chemicals and metallurgy industries, have reduced toxic discharges significantly, using new technology to treat waste water from saw mills, pulp mills and cardboard mills, and to remove heavy metals from industrial waste water.

There are also plans to clean up large harbours such as Montreal and Quebec City.

Tugs and harbour vessels are tied up in the port of Quebec.

Swimming is permitted in the St. Lawrence at several spots around Montreal.

Fish caught in Lake St. Francis are edible, but in limited quantities because some contain contaminants.

A whale watching boat crosses the foggy mouth of the Saguenay River.

Quebec City is the oldest port in Canada and, for most of its existence, there were no standards or laws to protect the environment. Shipping and industrial activity left several highly contaminated areas on the river bottom, including one area where 14 metres (46 feet) of pulp, wood shavings and fibres, mixed with minerals and heavy metals, had accumulated.

To safeguard wetlands and wildlife, migratory bird sanctuaries and other protected sites have been set aside, including sites on Lake St. François, Lake St. Pierre, Cap Tourmente and several islands. Established in 1904, St. Lawrence Islands National Park in the Thousand Islands is one of Canada's oldest national parks. Incorporating some 20 islands, 90 islets and a small base on the mainland, it is also the smallest. More recently the Saguenay-St. Lawrence Marine Park was established to protect the ecosystem of the fjord and the estuary. This 1,138-square kilometre (440-square mile) park is located entirely in a marine environment.

Tributaries are also being cleaned up. The Etchemin River near Quebec City, for example, was once one of the filthiest rivers in the province, with waste from saw mills and other industrial sources. Polluters have changed their ways, and now most of the remaining pollution in the Etchemin comes from agriculture. Small-mouth bass have returned to the river, and school children are raising salmon eggs in their classrooms and releasing the tiny fish into the river, in the hope that this will once again become a salmon spawning river.

Continual vigilance will be necessary, however, on the part of governments, industries and the public if the trend towards a cleaner St. Lawrence is to be maintained.

The Lake St. Pierre Biosphere Reserve features a vast wetland.

Three UNESCO Biosphere Reserves on the St. Lawrence

Three areas along the St. Lawrence River have been recognized by UNESCO as being particularly valuable ecologically and are now part of the World Network of Biosphere Reserves. As such, their landscapes and ecosystems are protected, sustainable development is encouraged, and support for research, monitoring and education are provided. The first area to achieve this distinction was the Charlevoix Biosphere Reserve, in 1988. This vast reserve is situated between St. Anne de Beaupré, east of Quebec City, and the Saguenay River, including both the coastal region and the interior mountains.

A 480-square kilometre (185-square mile) region of Lake St. Pierre, including the spring flood plain and important bird migration areas, was designated a Biosphere Reserve in 2000. Two years later the Thousand Islands-Frontenac Arch Biosphere Reserve was added to the list because of the high biodiversity of the area.

CHAPTER FOUR

Landscapes and Legends

The St. Lawrence has many moods – turbulent, capricious, placid, expansive – as it journeys to the sea. Its multifaceted character has inspired art in many forms: poetry, painting, photography, stories and songs, and the people who live along the river celebrate it in diverse ways.

Just as the St. Lawrence has four ecologically diverse stretches, it also inspires different traditions. The riverside communities of Ontario and upper New York State are steeped in stories about rum-runners, smugglers and romantic castles, cross-border skirmishes, running the rapids and monster muskellunges. The Mohawk, Innu and other aboriginal people have their own stories about "the road that walks."

The culture of French-speaking Quebec is closely linked to the river. The *Fleuve Saint-Laurent*, as it is known, is such a dominant feature of the landscape and such an important historical theme that it has been called the artery

The rugged north shore of the lower St. Lawrence is stunningly beautiful.

Montreal's international fireworks competition takes place beside the Jacques Cartier Bridge every summer.

Reddish sedimentary rocks are found all along the south shore of the estuary. These rocks are at Pointe au Père, facing southwest towards Rimouski.

and the soul of Quebec. In the estuary the rhythm of the tides governs comings and goings, the salt smells strong, the far shore is a faint line on the horizon and people refer to the river as *la mer* – the sea. Poets have said that Quebec has salt water in its veins. Today, however, many Quebecers are focused on contemporary urban issues, and the St. Lawrence appears infrequently as a theme in the arts.

Some communities are merely located on the river; others are of the river. Rimouski is such a place. Most of the commercial fishing vessels in the region call Rimouski home, and the college-level *Institut maritime du Québec* trains young people here for careers in navigation, diving, naval architecture and shipping security.

Nearby, Pointe au Père has an even closer connection to the St. Lawrence. The main ship-ping channel of the St. Lawrence was located on the river's south shore until 1959, so the light-house at Pointe au Père was crucially important. There was also a telegraph station there, and a pilot station where the pilots responsible for guiding vessels safely up and down the river transferred on and off the ships. Boats from Pointe au Père also ferried letters and parcels, transported there by rail, to ocean-going vessels in order to minimize transit time between Canada and Great Britain.

Today the telegraph station is closed, an automated lighthouse replaced the old structure in 1975, the pilot station moved to Les Escoumins on the north shore and the mail exchange boats are long gone. Nevertheless, people retain deep ties with the river. The 33-metre (108-foot) historic lighthouse, with its distinctive octagonal

Captain Paul de Villers, a retired river pilot who now lives in Lévis, Quebec, enjoys making model boats.

This charming oil painting of the village of Les Cèdres was made by an unknown artist around 1840, copying the style of well-known illustrator William Henry Bartlett.

shape and granite columns, is still a landmark, and the Musée de la Mer (museum of the sea) keeps alive the stories of navigation on the river and of the *Empress of Ireland*, the liner that sank offshore.

Landscapes

Many artists have been inspired by the river's natural beauty. Some of the first Europeans to portray it were military officers who recorded the sights they encountered in their travels. One of the first professional artists to draw the British colony was William Henry Bartlett, an English illustrator sent overseas by his publisher in 1838. He travelled from Quebec City to Niagara Falls, sketching boiling rapids, churches, marketplaces, native villages and waterfront scenes. After his return to England, he turned the sketches into steel engraving plates used to illustrate magazines and art journals. Some of his illustrations were somewhat fanciful, since most people preferred sentimental, picturesque scenes that were not necessarily representative of the still-untamed wilderness of North America. Nevertheless, Bartlett's prints were a hit at the time and remain popular today.

Artist Horatio Walker, born in Ontario in 1858, lived in New York and spent summers on Ile d'Orléans. Eventually he moved to the island full-time and painted the changing seasons, the tides and the *habitants* as they worked on their farms. Another artist, Clarence Gagnon, was also inspired by rural life along the lower St. Lawrence that he witnessed in the first half of the 20th century. Although he moved to Europe, he painted many landscapes from sketches he had made in Quebec.

A.Y. Jackson, a member of Canada's Group of Seven landscape painters, visited the lower St. Lawrence in the 1920's and found beauty in bleak autumn landscapes and windswept snow

Baie St. Paul has an active artistic community and numerous art galleries.

American artist Frederic Remington is best known for his illustrations of the American West, but he was also very familiar with the Thousand Islands region of upper New York State.

This mural on the side of a commercial building in Morrisburg, Ontario, was created by artist Cathie Cooper. This photo shows just a small detail of the mural.

This scene of a *habitant* home beside the St. Lawrence was painted by Adam Sheriff Scott.

scenes. Another Group of Seven member, Lawren Harris, made a famous painting of the lighthouse at Pointe au Père, while artist Marc-Aurèle Fortin often sketched Montreal's port, and Adam Sheriff Scott specialized in portraying historical subject matter. Many artists who were drawn to the river and its scenery lived in the Baie Saint Paul area, and this continues to be a busy artistic community today, with galleries that sell the works of a new generation of artists.

Ogdensburg was boyhood home to an artist who focused on a completely different subject: Frederic Remington's best-known works portrayed soldiers and the old American West, but in the last 10 years of his life he summered in the Thousand Islands, experimenting with colour as he interpreted the river's varying moods.

Ships of the St. Lawrence have inspired both artists and craftspeople. Canada Steamship Lines hired artists to memorialize its bulk carriers and otherwise unromantic vessels in beautiful settings, such as the St. Lawrence River near Quebec City. Perhaps the best-known image showed a bulk carrier sailing down Montreal's main business boulevard, dwarfing the cars and buses beside it.

Meanwhile untrained artists – many of them retired sailors or river pilots – paint simple, bright canvases of the schooners that once served the coast, or build models of the ships that were part of their working lives. Models of schooners, coastal freighters and other ships are lovingly detailed with tiny ladders, nets and portholes and usually constructed according to the designs of the original vessels.

In recent years a new trend toward art that is accessible to the public has appeared, with murals on the outsides of commercial and other buildings, depicting historical events and scenes of the river.

C.S.L. WHITEFISH BAY "SAILING" MONTREAL'S DORCHESTER BOULEVARD

MADE-TO-MEASURE, SEAWAY SIZE She's a lot of ship! Length: 730 feet; beam: 75 feet — the maximum limits for any vessel plying the

Seaway. And she carries a hefty cargo — 1,000,000 bushels of grain on the "down" trip, 25,000 tons of iron ore back up to the Great Lakes. The WHITEFISH BAY is

typical of Canada Steamship Lines' new fleet of Upper Lakes giants specially designed and built in its own Canadian shipyards for efficient, low-cost Seaway

service. This fleet, together with modern Canadian-built C.S.L. package freighters, moves a high proportion of the raw materials and finished products which

flow through this great inland artery. CANADA STEAMSHIP LINES LIMITED. Head Office: 759 Victoria Square, Montreal. Offices in principal Canadian cities.

Shipbuilding and Repairs   Heavy Industrial Equipment   Highway Transport   Heavy Lifting Services
Grain Elevators   Freight Terminals   Coal Docks   Warehouses   Resort Hotels & Cruise Ships

This imaginative scene of a 222-metre (730-foot) Canada Steamship Lines bulk carrier in the middle of a major thoroughfare in Montreal was created for a company advertisement. The Whitefish Bay was built at the Davie Shipyard, near Quebec City, in 1961 for service on the St. Lawrence Seaway.

Churches of the St. Lawrence

L'Église de Saint André is located in tiny Saint André de Kamouraska. Built in 1811, this church is classified as a historical monument and has a beautiful Mitchell organ.

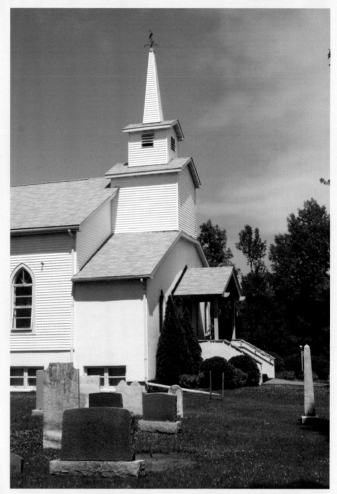

Salem United Church, dating from 1787, is on the banks of the St. Lawrence River at Summerstown, Ontario, a Loyalist community near Cornwall.

The back of Notre Dame de Bonsecours Chapel overlooks Montreal harbour. The church was first built in the 17th century and was reconstructed in 1771 following a fire. It is known as the sailor's church because parishioners used to pray there for loved ones at sea, and model ships donated by grateful sailors still hang from the chapel ceiling.

This Roman Catholic church, perched on a rise in St. Denis near Kamouraska, is typical of the stone churches found in villages along the south shore.

Visitors coming from the United States to Montreal often cross the St. Lawrence via the Champlain Bridge. The city is famous for its many great restaurants and annual events such as the Festival International de Jazz de Montréal.

The St. Lawrence in Song and Poem

Canadian folk music is full of river songs, such as rousing melodies about the timber-rafters who brought logs down the Ottawa River. Some of the old French songs that were popular with the *voyageurs* and *habitants*, such as *"À la claire fontaine,"* are still familiar today. The "Huron Carol," written by a missionary who lived with the aboriginal people in the 17th century, and *"Un Canadien errant,"* the tale of an exile who fled to the United States after the Rebellion of 1837, also remain very familiar to many Canadians.

Other songs, such as "A Canadian Boat Song," that were once heard everywhere, have now been forgotten. Its words were written in the 1830's by poet Thomas Moore and set to an old French tune he heard the boatmen sing while he travelled between Kingston and Montreal. One verse went:

> Faintly as tolls the evening chime
> Our voices keep tune and our oars keep time,
> Soon as the woods on shore look dim,
> Row, brothers, row, the stream runs fast,
> The Rapids are near and the daylight's past.

Some contemporary accounts of riverside life in early Canada remain well known. In 1852 Susanna Moodie, born to a refined family in England, wrote about her experiences as an immigrant arriving by ship and her pioneer life in Upper Canada in *Roughing It in the Bush*. Around the turn of the century, Ralph Connor, pen name of a Presbyterian minister, wrote lively novels about the Loyalist communities of Glengarry County on the upper St. Lawrence.

Kahnawake: at the Rapids

The Mohawk community of Kahnawake is just a few kilometres from downtown Montreal, on the south shore of the St. Lawrence River, but it is a world away from the big city. Kahnawake is a Mohawk word meaning "on the rapids," a reference to the nearby Lachine Rapids. Founded in the late 17th century, Kahnawake is a busy community of approximately 8,000 people on a 5,000-hectare (19-square mile) reserve administered by the Mohawk Council of Kahnawake, with local businesses, schools, radio stations and its own police service.

Offices of the Mohawk Council of Kahnawake are located in this modern building overlooking the St. Lawrence Seaway.

Many Mohawks have travelled across North America and abroad, working as ironworkers, constructing the steel ribs of office towers and bridges. Nevertheless, they have managed to keep much of their own culture alive. Many speak the Mohawk language, which is taught at local schools, and follow traditional spiritual beliefs, although Christian religions also have strong followings. Women hold significant political power, with family names and membership in clans being passed along from mothers to daughters. The Mohawks regard themselves as a sovereign nation, and the community is part of the Iroquois Confederacy, a historic alliance of Iroquois peoples.

Rafting through the Lachine Rapids is a thrilling experience.

Montrealers enjoy sailboat racing on Lake St. Louis.

The Shrine of St. Anne de Beaupré, east of Quebec City, attracts thousands of faithful worshippers.

Poet and editor Charles Sangster, one of the first writers to be inspired by wholly Canadian themes, made his mark with *The St. Lawrence and the Saguenay* in 1856. It was an extremely long poem – part love story, part travelogue – that described these rivers in picturesque detail.

One of the best-known novels to be set on the St. Lawrence River was *Le Survenant*, by award-winning author Germaine Guèvremont. In this 1945 book, the arrival of a stranger on an isolated island in Lake St. Pierre sets at least one heart aflutter. It was adapted for both radio and television in French. The English version, called *The Outlander*, made *The New York Times* best-seller list, and the newspaper's reviewer commented on the way the author successfully recreated a unique way of life while her characters reacted to universal situations. The story resurfaced in 2005 when it was made into a feature-length movie released in both French and English.

In the 1960's Quebec blossomed artistically, and poets and singer-songwriters became heroes of popular culture. Among the best known were Félix Leclerc and Gilles Vigneault, both of whom have close ties to the St. Lawrence. Vigneault was born in Natashquan, on the north shore of the gulf, while Leclerc died on his beloved Ile d'Orléans.

Destination St. Lawrence

The St. Lawrence River has been attracting visitors to its cool shores and rugged scenery ever since leisure travel became possible. In the early 1900's villages such as Tadoussac and Murray Bay were popular destinations. Many visitors travelled there by steamboat and stayed

CSL steamships carried passengers to and from the Manoir Richelieu Hotel at Murray Bay.

Thousand Islands Dressing

Believe it or not, the pieces of diced cucumber in Thousand Islands salad dressing are supposed to represent the islands of the real Thousand Islands. The story goes that one day, when hotel-owner George Boldt was aboard his yacht in the St Lawrence, he asked the chef to come up with something special. The chef created a dressing with the ingredients on board: some chopped green pickles and vegetables in a tangy sauce.

at hotels, such as the Hotel Tadoussac and the Manoir Richelieu Hotel, owned at the time by Canada Steamship Lines. The Hotel Tadoussac, with its trademark red roof, had its big moment in the spotlight when it appeared in the 1984 movie *The Hotel New Hampshire*. Today most visitors come by car or by bus, but these two hotels are still familiar landmarks.

Similarly the Chateau Frontenac Hotel, which dominates the skyline of Quebec City, was part of a chain of grand hotels across the country, built and operated by the Canadian Pacific Railway Company. Opened in 1893, it remains one of the country's best known hotels.

One of Murray Bay's most famous seasonal residents was William Howard Taft, who spent 30 summers at his cottage there, with a four-year break while he was president of the United

368 "ON THE BEACH" CACOUNA

Cacouna has been a summer resort for generations.

States. (He was later chief justice of the supreme court.) Many American tourists followed Taft to the Charlevoix to experience the region's charms for themselves.

The south shore of the lower St. Lawrence has also been a popular summer destination for several generations of Canadians. When there were no electric refrigerators or air conditioners to relieve the heat and humidity of Montreal, and diseases such as polio were still common in the crowded city, many families took the train to Rivière du Loup and spent their summers in the cool, salty air at nearby Cacouna, Notre Dame du Portage or Métis. Sir John A. Macdonald, Canada's first prime minister (1867-1873 and 1878-1891), and Louis Saint-Laurent, who was prime minister in the 1950's, both had riverfront homes in the region.

The Thousand Islands were attracting visitors by the late 1800's. Sports fishermen were the first to discover the area, and soon wealthy families began to build elaborate summer homes there. One of the area's most popular tourist attractions is the Boldt Castle, on the American side of the river. George Boldt, owner of the famous Waldorf Astoria Hotel in New York City, originally had this 120-room castle built for his wife, Louise. It was almost complete in 1904 when she died. Boldt immediately ordered a stop to construction and he never returned to the island. Now the castle and other buildings on the island have been renovated and opened to the public.

Today people enjoy the St. Lawrence River in many ways. Some like to view the water from shore, walking or cycling along its banks.

Families come to picnic on the beach below the steep sand dunes near Tadoussac.

Ice fishing is a popular winter sport on Lake St. François.

Tour guide Marys Plante describes the birds that are not visible through the fog surrounding the Brandy Pot Islands.

Abundant marine life attracts many divers to the waters of the Saguenay-St. Lawrence Marine Park.

Birdwatchers appreciate the river because it provides opportunities to watch great blue herons close to the city, to marvel at flocks of migrating geese or to catch sight of shy or unusual species. Sports fishermen can try their luck with a variety of species, including salmon on some tributaries. For those who want to get out on the water, sea kayaking is increasingly popular, especially in protected waters around the Thousand Islands, the many shallow bays along the south shore and along the rugged north shore.

For those who seek full immersion, the upper St. Lawrence is a scuba diver's paradise, with hundreds of wrecks to explore. Until a few years ago divers had to contend with poor visibility in the Thousand Island region, but zebra mussels have cleared the water and revealed new details of historic relics. Meanwhile the beauty and variety of marine life attracts divers to Les Escoumins, northeast of Tadoussac.

The two largest cities along the St. Lawrence, Montreal and Quebec City, also offer easy access to the waterfront, especially since obstructions such as grain elevators that once blocked views of the water have been removed and new parks have been developed along the shore. On warm summer days, Montrealers enjoy picnics beside the roaring Lachine Rapids or stroll beside the waterfront in the Old Port. Institutions such as the McCord Museum of Canadian History open windows on the river's past, and the Biodome of Montreal recreates the marine ecosystem of the St. Lawrence estuary indoors in a tidal pool stocked with sea anemones and starfish and an enormous salt water tank teeming with fish.

Quebec City, a UNESCO World Heritage Site and the only walled city north of Mexico, is like a living museum. There are reminders of the past around every corner, from Place Royale, heart of the first French settlement in the lower

Visitors inspect antique boats in Alexandria Bay, New York.

Built in 1872 as the home of the mayor of Gananoque, this building now serves as an inn.

The gardens of the Casino de Charlevoix in La Malbaie (Murray Bay) overlook the St. Lawrence.

The lawn of the Hotel Tadoussac is peaceful in the early morning light.

Notre Dame du Portage is a popular summer retreat near Rivière du Loup.

Visitors to the lower St. Lawrence experience the joy of empty sea and sky. This is the view from St. Siméon, northern terminus of ferry service to Rivière du Loup.

town, up the steep streets to Quebec's Parliament Hill. Avenue Royale, described as the *Route de la Nouvelle-France*, winds through the city's eastern suburbs where centuries-old houses, orchards and roadside crosses hug the hillside overlooking the river. Quebec City also offers many views of the river: from the promenade in the Old Port area, from the grassy parkland on the Plains of Abraham, from the ferry between Quebec City and south shore Lévis and from boat tours of the harbour.

Festivals Galore

People who live along the St. Lawrence celebrate river life in many ways. For example, Clayton, New York, home to a permanent antique boat museum, honours its shipbuilding heritage with an antique raceboat regatta. In Prescott, Ontario, Victoria Day celebrations in late May include an evening boat parade on the river and the blessing of the harbour during an outdoor religious service.

On an international scale, the Transat race takes place every four years between Quebec City and St. Malo, France, Jacques Cartier's home port. This sailboat race was first held in 1984 to celebrate the 450th anniversary of Cartier's arrival in North America. Participants come from Canada, the United States, France, Italy, Switzerland and Germany.

Winter is an inescapable fact of life on the St. Lawrence, but when the sun rises a little higher in the sky and the end of winter no longer seems hopelessly distant, people celebrate the season in style. The Quebec Winter Carnival, held in early February, is probably the most famous cel-

The Legend of *La roche pleureuse* ('the Weeping Rock')

In the collection *Légendes du Saint-Laurent II, récits des voyageurs*, Jean-Claude Dupont recounts this sad tale:

In May 1805, Charles Desgagnés readied his three-masted ship to carry a load of timber to the Old Country. He wanted to be home to marry his fiancée, Louise, before the end of September. After an evening of dancing, everyone said goodbye and the ship set sail.

Over the summer, Louise prepared the little house on the point of Ile aux Coudres where the couple would live. Soon, everything was ready, but when the leaves started to change colour in the autumn, she started to worry. Every afternoon she went down to the shore and sat on a rock, watching the horizon. Her father tried to reassure her that some ships lacked good winds and took longer than others to cross the Atlantic. Finally the snow came, and Louise scanned the horizon all day through the window.

In the spring, Louise started spending whole days on the point, talking quietly to herself and crying. One day she didn't return home. Her family and neighbours searched for her for days. Then, by the shore, her father noticed a trickle of water sliding down a rock amidst the wildflowers. He put his head on the rock for a minute, and then told everyone to stop searching. He realized Louise had turned into stone. Ever since then, she has been crying for her love, lost at sea.

ebration of winter in the world, with ice-sculpture competitions, parades and dozens of other events. The canoe race across the ice-strewn St. Lawrence is always one of the carnival's most popular events. Today this race is a test of strength and courage, but for generations, dangerous travel across the ice was a reality of life.

In the tiny village of St. Antoine de l'Isle aux Grues, residents hold a small but colourful festival to banish winter blues. For a week during the 40-day Lent period of penitence and fasting that leads up to Easter, the islanders throw a giant costume party, donning sequined, beribboned costumes and masks and going door-to-door in disguise. Called *mi-carême*, or mid-Lent, the event originated in medieval France, and this village is one of only a few places in Canada where it is still observed.

The canoe race across the St. Lawrence River is a popular event during Quebec City's annual winter carnival.

The Port Symphony offers hardy Montrealers a winter diversion.

Cross country skiers take advantage of an early snowfall on St. Helen's Island.

Creative landscaping, outdoor sculptures and floral festivals and displays, like this one in Old Montreal, splash colour along the banks of the St. Lawrence every summer.

Montrealers observe some maritime traditions of their own each winter. Port of Montreal officials present a gold-headed cane to the captain of the first ocean-going vessel to reach the port in the New Year. This tradition dates back to 1840, when the captain of the first vessel to reach the port without stopping en route generally arrived in late April or early May, heralding the beginning of the shipping season and bringing long-awaited mail from Europe. For the first 40 years of the tradition, the intrepid captain received a top hat; a gold-headed cane replaced the hat around 1880. Although the first ship of the year now usually arrives in the first few days of January, the ceremony is considered a tribute to all the captains and crews who make their way down the icy river each winter.

A more recent Montreal tradition is the Port Symphony, an event that takes place in late February in the Old Port area. Held annually since 1995, this event features a specially composed concert that incorporates the sounds of the horns of lakers wintering in the port, train locomotive whistles and church bells.

During one of the more sombre annual traditions, members of Montreal's Irish community remember the 6,000 people who died in the typhus epidemic of 1847. Most of the victims were poor Irish immigrants who never got a chance to make a new life in North America, but some of the nuns, priests and doctors who cared for them also died. In order to prevent the spread of the disease into the town, the sick were quarantined in sheds near the river, buried nearby and almost forgotten. When the Victoria Bridge was constructed, a large boulder was dredged from the river and erected on the shore to mark their graves. To this day, members of the Irish community "walk to the stone" and observe a brief service to remember those who died that terrible year.

Upper Canada Village in Morrisburg, Ontario, recreates life in the mid-1800s.

A variety of festivals and special events take place along the St. Lawrence during the summer months. Some are directly linked to the river, others merely take advantage of the spectacular venues it offers for activities ranging from outdoor concerts to food fairs. For example, singers and storytellers from around the world gather in south-shore Saint Jean Port Joli in August for a festival of maritime music. Cap Tourmente and Montmagny, in the upper estuary, celebrate the snow geese that visit their regions each fall. Gananoque celebrates island living each August with music, boat races and fireworks during the ten-day Festival of the Islands, and the Valleyfield Regatta, near Montreal, attracts thousands of speedboat racing fans every July.

Historic Heritage

The St. Lawrence is intimately linked with Canadian history. Thanks to its geography, it binds the past of Canada and the United States, and it links the fortunes of Ontario and Quebec. There are many places where people can become familiar with its heritage. Quebec City's old buildings and fortifications charm everyone, as does Upper Canada Village, the reconstruction of a mid-19th century village in Morrisburg, Ontario. Other legacies of the region's maritime heritage include the old lighthouse at Ile Verte and the Lachine Canal, which was opened to small pleasure craft in 2002.

Exhibits about life on the water can be found at the Marine Museum of the Great Lakes in Kingston, and the *Musée Maritime du Quebec* at

Expo '67

The biggest and best party ever held in Canada took place on the shores of the St. Lawrence River. It was 1967, the year Canada celebrated its 100th birthday, and the world was invited to Montreal to attend a world's fair, nicknamed Expo '67. The river provided a spectacular backdrop for the exhibits and performances held that magic summer.

Construction of the site began in 1964. Workers dredged millions of tons of mud from the riverbed and hauled rock to the site from tunnels being excavated for the city's new subway system (the Metro). This landfill was used to double the size of Ile St. Hélène (St. Helen's Island) and to build a brand new artificial island, Ile Notre Dame. Pavilions from dozens of countries, as well as exhibits that explored the fair's theme of Man and His World, were then constructed on the site. Canals and fountains surrounded the pavilions, reflecting their aluminum, steel mesh, concrete and glass shapes.

Nine years later, in 1976, Montreal hosted the summer Olympics, and again the river provided a backdrop for the "Big O," the concrete Olympic stadium built for the games. An inlet on Ile Notre Dame was used for the rowing events, while sailing races were held on Lake Ontario, near Kingston.

Today the Expo islands remain popular spots, especially in summer when Montrealers like to roam through the flower gardens, to spend a day at the amusement park or the beach, or to watch *L'International des Feux Loto-Québec*, the annual international

The British and French pavilions were amongst the most popular spots at Expo '67.

fireworks competition, on a warm evening. The geodesic dome structure that served as Expo's American pavilion, designed by architect Buckminster Fuller, is now called the Biosphere and houses exhibits focusing on water and environmental issues, including those facing the Great Lakes and St. Lawrence River. Meanwhile, Ile Notre Dame draws thousands of visitors to the casino, located in the former French pavilion, and plays host to the Grand Prix of Canada Formula 1 auto race each June.

Exhibits at Montreal's Biosphere teach visitors about the river. This building was originally the American pavilion at Expo 67.

A festival celebrates the legendary Pirate Bill Johnson every summer in Alexandria Bay.

The Reford Gardens (Jardins de Métis) in Grand Métis contain a vast array of plants and flowers from around the world and also host the International Garden Festival every year.

l'Islet sur Mer, on the estuary. The *Musée maritime de Charlevoix* in St. Joseph de la Rive focuses on the role that schooners played in the lower St. Lawrence. Military history is recalled at Fort Wellington near Prescott, the Stewart Museum at the fort on St. Helen's Island near Montreal, and at Coteau du Lac. Archaeological sites along the river shed light on early inhabitants and their cultures, and interpretation centres at Les Bergeronnes, near Tadoussac, Odanak, near Sorel, and Betsiamites, near Baie Comeau, offer insight into aboriginal traditions.

People also value the river's natural heritage. The Centre for the Interpretation of Marine Mammals in Tadoussac focuses on the whales found in the St. Lawrence, while numerous wildlife reserves along the river help protect environmentally sensitive areas.

The river has influenced people in many ways, although some may be more aware of it than others. Many residents of the lower St.

Tugboats mark a celebration in Montreal harbour.

Military drills are recreated on the grounds of The Stewart Museum on St. Helen's Island.

This memorial on the American side of the river is dedicated to people who work on the St. Lawrence.

In Anchor Park at Pointe des Cascades, west of Montreal, anchors, propellers and other ships' parts are on display.

Lawrence feel the river is in their blood. At least one member of almost every family seems to have worked on the river or in the shipyards, or to have sailed the Great Lakes and foreign seas. On the other hand, city dwellers are more likely to take the river for granted. When they sit in bumper-to-bumper traffic, trying to cross a bridge to get to work, it may seem more of an obstacle than a treasure.

But when they take the time to notice, they realize the St. Lawrence has bestowed a wonder-ful gift: diverse aquatic habitats, a rich history and an important commercial highway. As for the future of this river and its vast drainage system, it is up to citizens, businesses and governments to balance the various demands made on these resources and to ensure that waterways remain clean, healthy and beautiful for generations to come.

The Lost Villages Museum near Long Sault, Ontario, brings together buildings from the seven villages that were flooded to make way for construction of the St. Lawrence Seaway in the 1950's.

Quebec City is one of North America's oldest cities.

Rimouski is famous for its sunsets.

About the author

Janice Hamilton worked for six years as a reporter in the Montreal bureau of The Canadian Press. Since she began freelancing in 1984, her articles have appeared in numerous magazines, including *Canadian Geographic* and the *Canadian Medical Association Journal.* She has written more than 10 non-fiction books for children, including *Canadians in America* (Lerner Publications, 2006), a history of immigration between Canada and the United States. She regards herself as an amateur photographer and has taken numerous photography courses and workshops.

About the photographers

Derek Caron was a contributing photographer to Masterfile, Canada's largest photo stock agency, for 17 years and is an honorary life member of the Montreal Camera Club. He recently retired from a career in investment management.

Angèle Gagnon, whose family comes from the Baie St. Paul region, has been interested in photography for many years.

Kathlyn Horibe is a writer and editor whose photographs have been exhibited in Canada and the United States.

Barry McGee has been a full-time commercial, industrial and news photographer since 1960. He does nature photography for his own pleasure, taking advantage of the fact that the St. Lawrence is minutes from his house.

Harold Rosenberg freelanced as a news, sports and features photographer for *Maclean's* magazine and The Canadian Press, and was also a staff crime scene photographer for the Montreal police for 30 years.

Louise Tanguay is an award-winning nature photographer whose work has been featured in many magazines, newspapers and books.

Karen Thomson is an art consultant and teacher; her paintings can be found in collections in Canada, the U.S. and England.

Acknowledgements

First I want to thank my husband, Harold Rosenberg, with whom I had so much fun exploring this wonderful river. I must also thank Domenica diPiazza for getting me started on this project almost nine years ago, and publisher David Price for having the vision to bring it into reality.

I couldn't have done this without the wonderful photographs of Barry McGee and Derek Caron. Cecile Suchal, Joann Mitchell and Leslie Wagner were generous with professional advice, Cookie Kittredge and Anne Hardy gave feedback along the way, and Benny Beattie provided us with a place to stay in Tadoussac and shared his wealth of local knowledge.

Other experts who contributed to this book include archaeologist Michel Plourde, Patrice Corbeil of the Centre d'interprétation des mammifères marins, Ken Robinson of Parks Canada, Pascale Biron of Concordia University and Carolyn Eyles of McMaster University.

Among the many people who went out of their way to help me obtain photos were Bernard Collin and Denis Chamard of Fisheries and Oceans Canada, Normand Trudel of the Stewart Museum, Jennifer Scrimger of the Port of Montreal, Shiri Alon of the McCord Museum, Geraldine Fitzsimmons of the South Dundas Chamber of Commerce, Kathy Williamson of the Alexandria Bay Chamber of Commerce, Debbie Brentnell of Library and Archives Canada and Nicole Royer of Parks Canada. Thanks also to Denise Séguin and her colleagues at Environment Canada for the maps and artist Karen Thomson for the fish.

The mysterious and hardworking Ted Sancton also deserves thanks for putting everything together so beautifully.

The publisher would like to thank LG at PC and PC for their very generous support.

Map of Northeastern North America

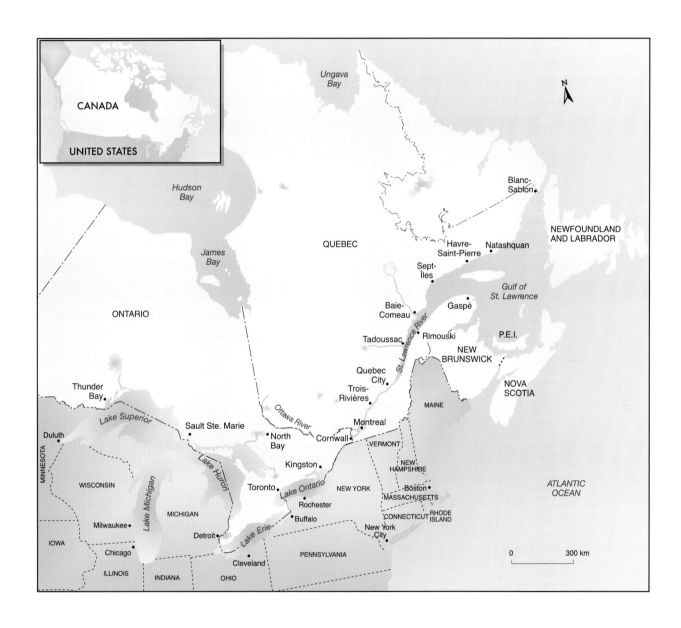

MAP   119

Map of the St. Lawrence River

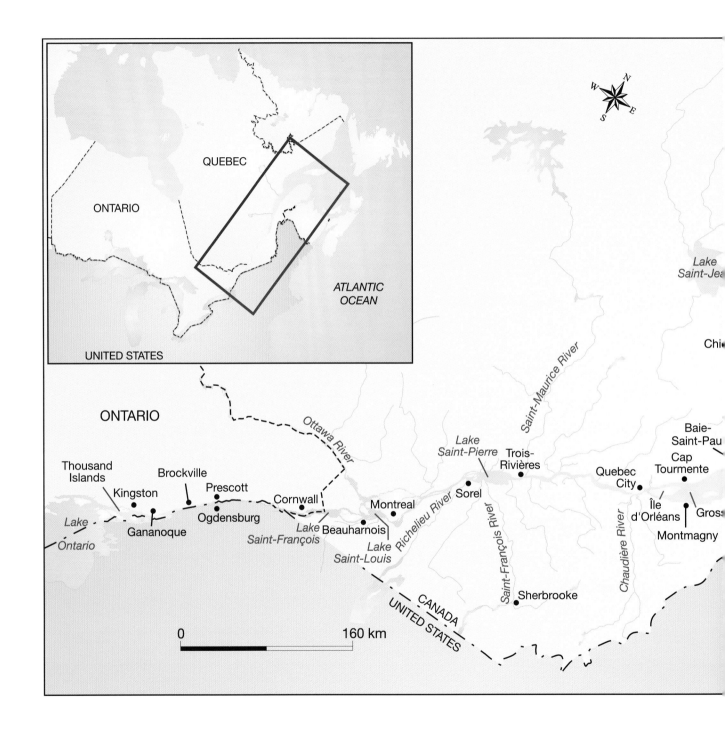

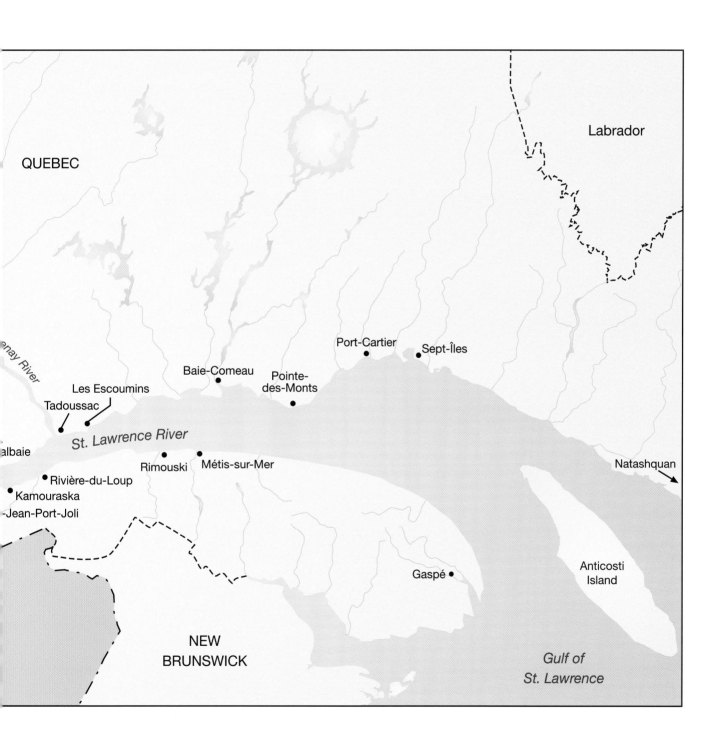

QUEBEC

Labrador

Port-Cartier
Sept-Îles

Baie-Comeau
Pointe-
des-Monts

Les Escoumins
Tadoussac

enay River

St. Lawrence River

albaie

Rimouski Métis-sur-Mer

Natashquan

Rivière-du-Loup
Kamouraska
-Jean-Port-Joli

Gaspé

Anticosti
Island

NEW
BRUNSWICK

*Gulf of
St. Lawrence*

MAP 121

Photo credits

Alexandria Bay Chamber of Commerce: 103 top, 112 top.

Archives nationales du Québec: 56 bot left: E6, S7, P2049-55.

Canada Steamship Lines: 93.

Canadian Coast Guard: 27 mid, 27 bot, 53 bot, 55 bot.

Derek Caron: cover, 4, 6, 9, 13, 14 top left, 16, 20 top, 20 bot, 24 top, 24 mid, 31 bot, 62, 74, 82, 83, 86, 88, 99, 108 bot, 109, 113 top, 113 bot, 115 bot, 116.

Centre d'interprétation des mammifères marins: 78 top, 78 bot.

Environment Canada, St. Lawrence Center, 2006: 119, 120.

Fisheries and Oceans Canada, D. Chamard: 53 top, 53 mid.

Angèle Gagnon: 94 left.

Janice Hamilton: 1, 8, 11 top, 11 bot, 14 top right, 14 bot left, 15, 17, 19, 21 mid, 21 bot, 22 top, 22 bot, 23 top, 23 bot, 24 bot, 26 top, 26 bot, 27 top, 28, 29 top, 29 mid, 29 bot, 30, 52 top, 55 top, 58 top, 58 mid, 58 bot, 60, 64 top, 64 bot, 65 top, 65 bot, 66, 67, 68 bot, 69, 70 top, 70 bot, 73 top, 73 bot, 79 bot, 81 top, 81 mid, 81 bot, 84 top, 84, mid, 84 bot, 89, 92 mid (permission South Dundas Chamber of Commerce), 94 right, 95 right, 97, 98 top, 102 top right, 102 bot right, 103 bot, 104 top, 104 bot, 105, 106, 107 bot, 111, 114 right, 115 top.

Kathlyn Horibe: 98 bot.

Hydro Québec: 12 top.

Library and Archives Canada: 32: C 002774 (detail); 34: C-041227 (detail); 35 top: C-000803 (detail); 35 bot: C-024163 (detail); 36: C-012750 (detail) 37 top: C-120844 (detail); 37 bot: C-011013 (detail); 38: C-010521; 40 top: C-011016 (detail); 40 bot: C-150399 (detail); 41 top: C-011859 (detail); 44 bot: C-013396 (detail); 45 bot: C-096362; 46 top: e002291741 (detail); 47 top: C 001029 (detail); 47 bot: C-000508 (detail); 48 top: C-040313 (detail); 48 bot: C-035271 (detail); 49 top: PA 122657 (detail); 51 top: PA 149728, 51 mid: C-022139 (detail); 51 bot: PA 008684 (detail); 52 bot: C-065396 (detail); 55 mid: C-002859 (detail); 56 top right: C-000214 (detail); 56 mid left: PA 126621; 56 mid right: C-115051 (detail); 56 bot right: PA 012789 (detail); 57 top: e000761666; 59: PA 118126 (detail); 90 bot: C-002739 (detail); 100 top: PA 069254, 101 top: PA 023503.

Barry McGee: 12 bot, 43 bot, 57 bot, 68 top, 71, 79 top, 80, 85, 96, 108 top, 110.

Musée de la Mer: 54.

Notman Photographic Archives, McCord Museum of Canadian History: 50 bot: 1-76310; 56 top left: V8828.

Parks Canada: 49 mid, 49 bot, 76 top, 76 bot, 77, 102 bot left.

Photo Librarium Canada: 10 top, 10 bot, 21 top, 43 top, 107 top.

Port of Montreal: 25 top, 25 bot.

Harold Rosenberg: 14 bot right, 18, 31 top, 61, 75, 90 top, 91, 92 bot, 95 left, 102 top left, 114 left.

Stewart Museum: 39, 41 bot, 42, 44 top, 45 top, 46 bot, 50 top, 92 top.

Louise Tanguay: 112 bot.

Karen Thomson: 72.

Selected Sources and Recommended Reading

Beattie, Benny. *Tadoussac: The Sands of Summer.* Montreal: Price Patterson Ltd., 1994.

Camu, Pierre. *Le Saint Laurent et les Grands Lacs au temps de la voile, 1608-1850.* LaSalle: Hurtubise HMH, 1996.

Collard, Edgar Andrew. *Passage to the Sea. The Story of Canada Steamship Lines.* Toronto: Doubleday Canada Ltd., 1991.

Dupont, Jean-Claude. *Légendes du Saint-Laurent, II. Récits des voyageurs, de l'Île-aux-Coudres à l'Île d'Anticosti.* Sainte-Foy: Les Éditions J.-C. Dupont, 1985.

Environment Canada. *Environmental Atlas of the St. Lawrence. A River, Estuaries, and a Gulf. Broad Hydrographic Divisions of the St. Lawrence.* 1991.

Environment Canada. St. Lawrence Centre. HTTP://WWW.QC.EC.GC.CA/CSL/INF/INF001_E.HTML

Environment Canada. *The River at a Glance. Info-flash on the State of the St. Lawrence River.* Saint-Laurent Vision 2000. 1997.

Francis, R. Douglas; Jones, Richard; Smith, Donald B. *Origins: Canadian History to Confederation.* Toronto: Holt, Rinehart and Winston of Canada, 1988.

Franck, Alain. *Naviguer sur le fleuve au temps passé: 1860-1960.* Sainte Foy: Les Publications du Québec, 2000.

Gagné, Jean. *À la découverte du Saint-Laurent.* Montréal: Les Éditions de l'Homme, 2005.

Greenfield, Nathan M. *The Battle of the St. Lawrence: the Second World War in Canada.* Toronto: Harper Collins Publishers Ltd., 2004.

Hamilton, Janice. *Destination Montreal.* Minneapolis: Lerner Publications, 1997.

Historica. The Canadian Encyclopedia. WWW.THECANADIANENCYCLOPEDIA.COM

Jenkins, Phil. *River Song: Sailing the History of the St. Lawrence.* Toronto: Viking, 2001.

Lafrenière, Normand. *Lightkeeping on the St. Lawrence.* Toronto: Dundurn Press, 1996.

Lefolii, Ken. *The St. Lawrence Valley.* The Illustrated Natural History of Canada. Toronto: NSL Natural Science of Canada Limited, 1970.

Morrison, R. Bruce; Wilson, C. Roderick, eds. *Native Peoples: The Canadian Experience, 2nd ed.* Toronto: McClelland & Stewart, 1995.

Parks Canada. National Historic Sites of Canada. HTTP://WWW.PC.GC.CA/PROGS/LHN-NHS/INDEX_E.ASP

Provencher, Jean. *Les Quatre Saisons dans la vallée du Saint-Laurent.* Montreal: Les Éditions du Boréal, 1996.

Ray, Arthur J. *I have Lived Here Since the World Began.* Toronto: Lester Publishing and Key Porter Books, 1996.

Rhealt, Pascal-Andrée; Gaudreau, Gilles. *Itinéraire et découvertes culturelles au Bas-Saint-Laurent.* Trois Pistoles: Centre d'édition des Basques, 1999.

Ross, Don. *St. Lawrence Islands National Park.* Vancouver: Douglas & McIntyre, 1983.

Saint Laurent Vision 2000. Biodiversity Portrait of the St. Lawrence. HTTP://WWW.QC.EC.GC.CA/FAUNE/BIODIV/

Saint-Laurent Vision 2000. Information about the St. Lawrence River. HTTP://WWW.SLV2000.QC.CA/INDEX_A.HTM

St. Lawrence Centre. *State of the Environment Report on the St. Lawrence River. Volume 1. The St. Lawrence Ecosystem.* Montreal: Environment Canada, Quebec Region, Environmental Conservation, and Éditions Multimondes, 1996.

Ten Cate, Adrian G. *A Pictorial History of the Thousand Islands.* Brockville: Besancourt, 1977.

Thompson, Shawn. *A River Rat's Guide to the Thousand Islands.* Erin, Ontario: The Boston Mills Press, 1996.

van der AA, Hans. *Gateway to the World: a picture story of the St. Lawrence Seaway.* Montreal: Chomedy Publications, 1959.

Villeneuve, Claude; Back, Frédéric. *Le fleuve aux grandes eaux.* Montréal: Les éditions Québec/Amérique, 1995.

Zeni, David. *Forgotten Empress: The Empress of Ireland Story.* Fredericton: Goose Lane Editions, 1998.

Index

Montreal guidebooks that you might find useful:

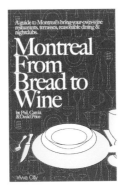

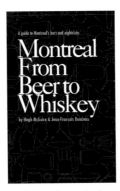

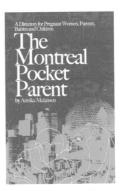

A Montreal Gazette
bestseller (#2 August 6,
2005); 7 weeks on list

A brand new look
at the Montreal
bar scene.

An indispensable
guide for parents
in Montreal.

Other guidebooks from Vivva City that you might enjoy:

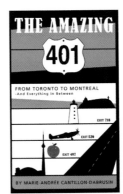

A small book packed
with useful
information.

A fun and helpful look
at the 401, for veterans
and newcomers to
Ontario's premier
highway.